MORE THAN A
FISHERMAN

OTHER BOOKS BY
DR. JAMES GRASSI

Guts, Grace, and Glory
The Ultimate Men's Ministry Encyclopedia
A Study Guide of Israel
Crunch Time
Crunch Time in the Red Zone
Wading Through the Chaos
The Ultimate Hunt
In Pursuit of the Prize
Heaven on Earth
The Ultimate Fishing Challenge
The Spiritual Mentor
Building a Ministry of Spiritual Mentoring

Men's Ministry Catalyst Website:
www.mensministrycatalyst.org

MORE THAN A FISHERMAN

BY JIM **GRASSI**

Thomas Nelson
Since 1798

NASHVILLE   DALLAS   MEXICO CITY   RIO DE JANEIRO

Published in Nashville, Tennessee, by Thomas Nelson. Thomas Nelson is a registered trademark of HarperCollins Christian Publishing, Inc.

Page Design and layout: Crosslin Creative

Images: Jim Grassi, Yoel Ben-Yosef, Beit Haoganim (The House of Anchors) Museum at Kibbutz Ein Gev, Sea of Galilee, Israel

Thomas Nelson, Inc. titles may be purchased in bulk for educational, business, fund-raising, or sales promotional use. For information, please e-mail SpecialMarkets@ThomasNelson.com.

This book is dedicated to those who wish to grow into an authentic disciple of Jesus Christ. He is and was and shall ever be. Let us absorb the teachings of the Master Fisherman to His disciples so that we obtain a greater understanding of what it means to know God and make Him known. The command "Follow Me, and I will make you fishers of men" (Matt. 4:19) is a call to become a *fisher of men*. With the power of the Holy Spirit, we can be a change agent within our culture.

Author Jim Grassi believes that we need to connect with younger generation (Bryson Mort)

CONTENTS

FOREWORD

Jim Grassi is not only a Hall of Fame Fisherman but a true fisher of men. He has taken biblical truth and connected some great metaphors that help all of us to know God and make Him known. We need to be authentic followers of Jesus, and in this unique work Jim helps us explore the words of Christ to his disciples.

Before I became a Christian I asked myself what was so powerful about Jesus' teaching that transformed men into being committed followers who were willing to die for their faith. Why did Jesus choose eight fishermen of the original twelve disciples to be his followers?

Anyone who knows me understands that I endeavor to bring passion into whatever I do. In his unique work *More Than a Fisherman,* Jim helps us understand what it means to be a spiritual mentor and the passion God wants us to have about our faith. We become better in whatever we do when we have a guide to show us the way. This simple but profound book helps us see the essence of discipleship from the eyes of his first-century disciples.

I love story—especially good fishing stories. From his own experiences, and the lives of some fishing legends, Jim motivates us to think about discipleship from a fresh perspective. Each chapter opens a topic that requires the reader to explore his faith and commitment to Jesus.

Al Lindner
Director, Lindner Media Productions
Host: *Angling Edge/Fishing Edge* TV

INTRODUCTION

For the most part, men are visual learners. If you can't show them an illustration, the next best thing is to paint a word picture so that they can connect the thought to a metaphor or anecdote. This book utilizes a number of pictures, graphics, and stories that will help the reader to remember and apply biblical truth to their lives. Many good Bible teachers and coaches use visualization techniques to help people remember and better understand what can be complex issues and situations. Jesus, the greatest teacher of all, regularly used illustrations to help people experience the depth of His passion and to help them relate His teachings to their lives. Enjoy the adventure of knowing the heart of Jesus through story and illustrations.

One of my favorite fishing memories comes from my first trip to New Zealand. I was filming a project for the New Zealand Tourism Bureau, which had scheduled me to do some ultra-light fishing from the top of the North Island to the bottom of the South Island. At 5:00 a.m. on the first fishing day, a local guide named Captain Ed knocked on my motel room door and said, "Jim, let's get rollin', time is a wasting. If we don't get to my spot in a timely manner we will miss the opportunity." As tired as I was from all the travel the day before, I knew from the urgency in his voice that I'd better get dressed and out to his truck as soon as possible.

Captain Ed took me out to a shallow reef near the Bay of Islands, where I witnessed a scene I'll never forget. As we quietly pulled up to a rocky point and shut down the outboard engines, there was an explosion of fish on the surface. It was as if someone had turned up the heat on a saucepan full of popcorn kernels. Fish of all sizes were in a feeding frenzy and popping up all over the bay.

Thousands of fish were boiling to the surface as the captain told our video crew that they had better get their cameras rolling. He then barked out orders for me to get my lures in the water because this unique event would be over in about an hour. I was like a kid catching his first fish on a pond loaded with hungry bluegill. I couldn't make up my mind whether to use my fly rod or ultra-light spinning rod. Feeling the urgency, I grabbed both before I realized that I could only use one at a time. After catching and releasing over forty fish in an hour, the fish disappeared. The captain said, "That's it for today, Jim." Wow! As the surge of adrenaline began to leave my body, I sank back into the reality that I may never again experience that kind of adventure.

Throughout His ministry, Jesus told His disciples to become passionate and persistent and prayerful about those who were lost. He regularly reminded His followers that they were the salt and light of the world (Matt. 5:13–16). He expressed to them that there was an *urgency* about learning how to disciple others. He knew His time was limited and even told the disciples that He would not always be with them (John 7:33).

The apostle Paul expressed a similar urgency to preaching the gospel when he penned these words: "But all things that are exposed are made manifest by the light, for whatever makes manifest is light. Therefore He says: 'Awake, you who sleep, arise from the dead, and Christ will give you light'" (Eph. 5:13–14).

My friend, there is an urgency to getting a message of hope to a lost generation. Our government reminds us regularly of the vulnerability that we face with the possibility of a terrorist attack. Current events in the Mideast suggest that world peace is an illusion. With the continual moral decline of our country and the increase in the fulfillment of biblical prophecy, it is appropriate that we see Christ's return as imminent. While we should not predict a time of His return, clearly the prophetic signs point to the fact that we are living in the last days. The Bible tells us, "But we are not of those who draw back to perdition, but of those who believe to the saving of the soul" (Heb. 10:39).

Many would say that it's not politically correct to discuss religion with people outside the church. Forget about being politically correct—let's consider the fact that souls are at stake and we need to share the hope and love of Christ with those whom God puts before us. As the Holy Spirit directs, be available to share the truth of your salvation. In Romans 11:25, Paul tells us, "For I do not desire, brethren, that you should be ignorant of this mystery, lest you should be wise in your own opinion, that blindness in part has happened to Israel until the fullness of the Gentiles has come in." The "fullness of the Gentiles" suggests that the time when to world is ripe for our Lord to return will be signaled by events or even completing the conversion of those called by God. Obviously the believers have a role to play here that brings the present age to a close. It follows that the quicker we can share the good news to the lost, the faster they can be led by the Holy Spirit to accept Jesus as their Savior and this time we are in will be complete.

Using fishing as a metaphor, it is my desire to share with you what I and millions of others have found to be *true and right*: a personal relationship with Jesus Christ. It matters not if you are a fisherman or even care about fishing (although there are about forty million anglers in this country); what is important is that you connect with the anecdotes to see how God's Word can be applied to your approach to discipleship (spiritual mentoring). One of the tragedies of our Christian culture is that most believers either are fearful to share their faith or do not know how. It is my prayer, through these words, illustrations, and the power of the Holy Spirit within you, that you will realize that being a spiritual mentor of others doesn't require a PhD or seminary degree; it is so simple that even a child can do it.

I define a spiritual mentor as someone who disciples another through the use of relational platforms so as to fully connect with the person being mentored. Being a spiritual mentor is ultimately about building a relationship that can help both parties become stronger in their faith. If we agree that the most precious of gifts is *time*, then the idea of investing in others or having someone invest in you is a special thing. It implies the heart of discipling another person within the context of a relational mentoring environment. That is to say, the most effective and long-lasting discipling relationships happen best when you seek to encourage and equip the person in areas beyond just the spiritual aspects of life. If you can find common interest areas, such as sports, hobbies, cultural interests, work, or family, your relationship will have dimensions that will help hold you together during trying times.

My good friend Phil Downer, founder and president of Discipleship Network of America, has spent his life investing in men. In his solid work *Eternal Impact*, he described for us the importance of the spiritual concept of *iron sharpening iron* (Prov. 27:17), one man helping another.

> That is exactly what many people need today—others to walk with them, offering wisdom and encouragement, particularly in difficult times. Men in our work are in turmoil. The pressures of our modern age are draining away the joy and leaving people too exhausted to experience the abundant life God has promised. They are physically tired, emotionally drained, overwhelmed by debt, and trying to cope with damaged relationships.[1]

In Thomas Nelson's book series titled *A Romans 12 Disciple*, I have written several books designed for men. In my mind, men are the key operatives if there is any hope for a spiritual reformation in this country. As mentioned in the first two books, when men accept Jesus as their Savior and Lord, 93 percent of the time they will impact their families and those around them.[2] If ever there was a time when men need to be transparent and passionate about their faith, it is now.

Transformational male friendships are those that happen when spiritual matters and accountability are part of the conversation. Relational encounters that have transformation as an end goal become important in the process of spiritual development. When people work on transforming their lives into the likeness of Christ, they are better equipped to pray for and assist others who seek to become spiritually mature. As Jesus modeled care, compassion, strength, and discernment to His followers, we need spiritual mentors who can assist with dynamic life changes.

In several places within the New Testament, when Jesus called His disciples, He used the expression, "Follow Me, and I will make you fishers of men." A modern-day translation would be, "Let's go fishing." Fishing for souls requires commitment and dedication. It requires guys willing to care enough to explore new ways of casting their spiritual nets to those who are lost. So let's go fishing!

IT'S **TIME**
TO **FISH**

FISHING TALE

It was a late summer day when our family met some close family friends on a famous blue ribbon trout river called Hat Creek. Hat Creek is a long stream located in Northern California, and the crystal-clear water and shallowness of the stream presents a real challenge to even the most talented trout fisherman. This is a catch-and-release waterway with an abundance of bug life, so trout grow to trophy size in no time.

Perhaps the most noteworthy aspect of this unique regional fishery is the giant *Hexagenia* (*hex*) mayflies that hatch from their watery cocoons every year. For some strange reason, these bugs hatch out in the evening right at dusk. These insects are almost as large as the small bats that are flying about eating them as they emerge from the water.

Fly fishermen live by a slogan of "matching the hatch." When fishing in the late evening while you can still see your tackle box, pick out a couple of large flies that look like the hatch coming off the water. If you are able to get your fly into the water before a bat captures it, you will see some of the most exciting dry-fly trout fishing action in the United States. Large trout wait for this time in the evening to gorge themselves with these meaty bugs. The fish are tenacious and aggressive, which makes them vulnerable as they slurp down these giant bugs for a prime dinner.

Fishing with a cast net. 19th century drawing. Source: thewikibible.pbworks.com

The main problem with this type of fishing is seeing your equipment and flies. This isn't the time to mess up a cast. One needs to be able to carefully and patiently pursue his quarry with little or no light. To turn on a flashlight in order to straighten out your leader or tie on another fly spells disaster. Once the light hits the water, the fish stop biting. Any western fly fisherman with a knowledge of this stream knows that, when the *hex* hatch is on, there will be great fishing. As difficult as it is, the reward is great. In a like manner, discipling others at times can certainly be difficult, but it also has tremendous rewards.

CASTING FOR THE TRUTH

When walking along the shoreline at the Sea of Galilee, Jesus offered a life-changing challenge to a group of unlettered but respected fishermen. He wanted them to consider the call—but not without *counting the cost*. Jesus said, "Follow Me, and I will make you fishers of men" (Matt. 4:19). In saying "Follow Me," Jesus was asking each fisherman to follow and believe in Him. As He spoke the words "I will make you fishers of men," He was informing them that He would give them a ministry and purpose for their lives.

Unlike a fisherman whose catch merely yields something to eat or brag about, Jesus wanted His disciples to think about catching men's hearts with a provocative and life-changing message. The goal was to empower, train, equip, and release these men for service. Jesus' words and actions affirmed a message that, unlike fishing for fish, it is never out of season to fish for souls.

The discipleship concept worked well in the first century, and it continues to work today. The disciples didn't just learn from Jesus and stop there. They went out and *taught others* what they learned. Despite the many similarities between fishing for fish and fishing for men, there is a key difference as well. Jesus indicated to Peter, a seasoned fisherman, that from now on he would be taking men alive (Luke 5:1–11) and releasing them to change the world. Peter Marshall, twice chaplain of the US Senate, illuminated this passage when speaking at the University of Pittsburgh in 1946: "Fishing for fish is pulling fish out of life into death. Fishing for men is pulling them out of death into life."[1]

A good fisherman will evaluate the water he is fishing so he can select the right equipment. A pond will be fished differently than the ocean. So it is with a discipler of men, or what I call a spiritual mentor. We need to understand our culture and then we can apply what we know of God's Word. The following statistics demonstrate the extreme urgency to reach men in today's world.

* There are 69 million men who make no profession of faith in Christ.

* Fatherless children are five times as likely to live in poverty, repeat a grade, and have emotional problems.

* Only 1 out of 18 men in America is involved in active discipleship.

* As many as 70 percent of men have actively sought out pornography this year.

* Ninety-three percent of all people incarcerated are men, and 85 percent of them have no father figure.

* As many Christians will divorce as non-Christians.

* Most men only know enough about God to be disappointed with Him.

✳ Too many men daily fight depression, loneliness, and despair with little hope to change their perspective.[2]

What is at stake? It has been said, "As goes the family, so goes the nation." Our government has invested billions of dollars to help shape the nation's educational system and social networks. Our liberal media believes that it is more important to be "politically correct" than to uphold the values of decency and truth. Our social, economic, and political systems seem to lack reverence and respect for the biblically based ideals our founding fathers identified in our governing documents.

Kenneth Bradwell, executive director of Fathers Incorporated, has stated that there are "millions of children in the United States who wake up each morning without a biological father in the home. Today, these children represent 24 million and the number is growing—and growing disproportionately in Black and Latino families."[3] As I said in my book *The Spiritual Mentor*, when you contemplate this disturbing statistic, it is not a mystery why so many kids are prone to juvenile delinquency, teen pregnancy, sexual identity issues, school difficulties, and more. More than ever before, we need capable, strong men of God to disciple their kids and to become the spiritual leaders within their families, churches, and communities. One could say, "As goes the husband or father, so goes the family, church, or government." Again, it starts with relationships. Mentoring, discipling, and modeling cannot be replaced with governmental mandates or a social gospel.

And it all begins with men who want to grow in their faith. This book is about challenging men to dig deeper into their faith and convictions and then be courageous to act on them. Hopefully you will see some revolutionary ideas and an amplified theology on the most important challenge given to mankind by our dear Lord and Savior: *Go make disciples.*

Have we lost our way by listening to slick theological and socially accepted arguments? Are we attending churches that are more interested in the "show" or entertaining us rather than helping us transform our lives into the likeness of Christ? Too many churches have had their focus on the size of their congregations instead of on the spiritual depth of their members. The emphasis has been on the three "B's"—budgets, baptisms, and buildings. If there is a saving grace for the church today, it will be because people like you and me care enough about discipleship that we get out of our complacency and self-centered attitudes and join the most important battle ever fought. No longer must we look at our spiritual development as something that we "catch" or "fall into." Instead, we are to be soldiers ready for action in the battle for men's souls. A true disciple, then, will have a sincere belief *and* resulting action if he is going to be effective in reaching others for the kingdom.

WHAT MAKES A GREAT FISHER OF MEN?

There are various types of fishermen and disciples, and they seem to fall into one of several different camps. As you think about your responsibility of being a follower of Christ, where do you see yourself in this list of fishermen?

* Those who think about fishing: Philosophers

* Those who study about it and stay at home and never see a lake or stream: Scholars

* Those who stand on the shore and watch others fish: Observers

* Those who go through the motions but believe that their equipment isn't really good enough: Pretenders and Deceivers

* Those critical of the whole idea of fishing: Destroyers

* Those who write a check to enable others to fish: Sponsors

* Those who partake of the meal after the fish are caught: Freeloaders, Ticks, and Parasites

* Those who pursue the sport with passion and zeal: Disciples[4]

LET'S GO FISHING

In over three decades of ministry to men, I've never seen so many men dealing with major challenges as I do today. Those challenges bring a host of opportunities to share our faith and to encourage others in their spiritual journey. Much like my experience on Hat Creek, there is an urgency connected with the opportunity. Men are seeking peace, love, joy, and real relationships. They endeavor to make some sense out of the mess we are in. Only God's Word can direct us to answers that will change our lives and stabilize our thinking about how to cope in this stress-filled world.

In order to reach others for God's kingdom, we need to consistently employ the gifts, talents, and contacts the Lord has provided us with. The twenty-first-century church must be practical and relevant to the world in which we live. Men must be willing to embrace their roles as spiritual leaders and commit themselves to the personal involvement that discipleship requires.

From the first-century disciples, we also learn that effective discipleship requires grace and patience that only God can provide. German clergyman Dietrich Bonhoeffer informed us that "when we are called to follow Christ, we are summoned to an exclusive attachment to his person. . . . The call goes forth, and is at once followed by the response of obedience. . . . Christianity without discipleship is always Christianity without Christ."[5]

FISHING FOR MEN

Spend time reading Luke 5:1–11 together with your mentoring partner. Summarize what this passage is saying in your own words. What risks did Peter take? If you had been in Peter's place, a long-seasoned fisherman on the Sea of Galilee, how would you have responded to Jesus' command? What does this passage teach you about yourself and God?

THE
FIRST-CENTURY
FISHERMEN

FISHING TALE

Shortly after leaving His hometown of Nazareth, Jesus came down the hillside to a little settlement called Capernaum. As He strolled along the Sea of Galilee shoreline, He came upon a small group of fishermen who had been with John the Baptist. These were special men who knew the challenges life brings. Being a fisherman for a small Galilean settlement (Kibbutz) was not an easy task. With meat being scarce, fish was one of the main staples in the diet for people who lived in this community.

Peter and Andrew were brothers, as were James and John, the sons of Zebedee. Zebedee owned the fishing boat (27 feet long by 7.5 feet wide) and, since we don't hear more about him, we must assume that he was not part of the fishing excursions we find in the New Testament. If you look at John 21, you will note that, besides John, we can identify seven other disciples who were most likely fishermen.

This raises the question, why did Jesus choose fishermen? Practically speaking, the fishermen-disciples had efficient transportation and the ability to provide meals for the group, but I believe Jesus saw in these men traits that set them apart as good candidates to be the first-century disciples.[1]

A fisherman for a small community like Kibbutz would go out in his boat just before dark and set a small fire in a polished brass pan. The light from the fire attracted small fish to the boat. He would cast his net into the dark shadows of the night, only to quickly retrieve it before it sank to the bottom. Often, the cold night air would penetrate his wet clothes and cause his body temperature to fall. There was always the worry that a wind storm would come up, washing him and his equipment onto the rocky shoreline. (The Sea of Galilee is notorious for sudden, violent storms.) The stink from the previous day's catch still lingered in the old wooden boat, as he and his partners gingerly stepped over the freshly caught, slimy fish jumping about the boat. This was a job not for the faint of heart, but for men who were willing to risk it all for the sake of others. What are you willing to risk in becoming a fisher of men?

THE FIRST-CENTURY FISHERMEN

In researching and writing *Promising Waters*, I was struck with the numerous parallels and correlations that exist between the fishermen and fishers of men. These simple Galilean fishermen were rough and somewhat pedestrian in their thinking. Their Jewish roots, filled with passion and prejudice, often presented challenges to learning new ideas. Despite their obvious skill and success in the fishing community, these practical, hard-working men would soon give up their musty nets and smelly fish to catch the vision of Christ's ministry.

Jesus wanted to relate to men who understood the challenges of life in a unique way, men who dealt with the mysteries of nature. He could have gone to the intellectuals, the elite, or the Pharisees or Sadducees, but He picked common guys who weren't handicapped by their pride or seeking materialistic goods. He realized that many of the principles, methods, and techniques used in relating to people on a spiritual basis are very similar to those used in fishing. By learning how to apply Jesus' teachings, the disciples could then pursue the ultimate fishing challenge: becoming fishers of men. Jesus wanted to lead them on the fishing adventure of a lifetime, where the rewards have eternal consequences with net-breaking excitement.

In the first century, an apprenticeship system was used to train spiritual leaders. Those in training attached themselves to a rabbi and literally lived with him. Their goal was both to learn all their teacher knew and to imitate his way of life. When Barnabas found Paul, he became his spiritual mentor. Paul learned from Barnabas how important it was to have someone in his life who was spiritually mature. As a consequence, Paul found a young man named Timothy who needed counsel from someone a little further along in his spiritual journey. These men served as models for one another and continued to pass on the legacy of their faith (Acts 15:22–23; Gal. 2:1–10)

As I researched the word *disciple*, I found that two elements apply. One must have a certain attitude and resulting actions if he is to be a true disciple. The Greek word for disciple is *mathetes* (root word is *manthano*), which simply means "to learn." Therefore, a *mathetes* is a "learner, pupil, or student." But if the disciple did not apply what he learned, he could not be counted as a believer. The greatest honor you can give your Master is to share with others the joy of your experience and understanding.

It is curious how many comparisons there are between fishermen and fishers of men. Perhaps when Jesus was thinking about the manifested traits of fishermen he realized these were the guys to passionately carry his message.

Fishermen are a *unique breed* and are rarely understood by others. More often than not, they are considered a little odd or eccentric. Likewise, fishers of men don't always lend themselves toward a neat, ecclesiastical job description; however, they do have some common characteristics.

Fishermen are *inquisitive* people of adventure and exploration; a disciple is never content with the routine and the mundane. Fishermen keep *focused* on what they are doing and how that impacts their approach to the fish; a disciple fixes his eyes on men who are more advanced in their spiritual development and uses his Spirit-filled life to tackle each challenge and embrace each relationship as an opportunity to serve our Lord.

Fishermen have *faith* that every cast will produce a fish. They believe that just one more cast will be "the one." Fishers of men live by faith, not by sight (2 Cor. 5:7). This is the same faith Peter demonstrated when he cast his bare hook into the Sea of Galilee and caught a fish with a coin in its mouth (Matt. 17:27).

Committed fishermen are *passionate* and *persistent*. They will spend countless hours preparing, analyzing, evaluating, and pursuing their beloved sport. They challenge the fish and don't give up. Similarly, a devoted disciple of Jesus attacks his mission with the same dedication and zeal.

Fishermen are people of *skill* and *knowledge*. They know and study the habits and habitats of the fish while routinely practicing their casting skills. They take the necessary time to prepare for their fishing adventure. Likewise, fishers of men understand the sin-filled environment in which they live and work, while carefully devoting themselves to preparatory prayer and study.

Fishermen are eager to *share* their knowledge, experiences, and skill with others. Whether it's a new lure or favorite fishing hole or just bragging about the fish you caught, we love to tell stories. Storytelling is important to helping people come to a practical understanding of our Lord and how He can help us sort out life. Believers are equally interested in sharing the joy of our Lord and Savior with others.

Fishermen take *risks* and *overcome* the obstacles before them. As commented on earlier, there were many risks in belonging to the order of Galilee fishermen. Most fishermen have experienced the reward that comes from persevering and pursuing fish. As we saw in Luke 5, the disciples were challenged with casting their nets in the middle of the day as the Lord directed. It was a risk of embarrassment, because they knew that most fish were not caught at midday. They soon recognized that a more difficult challenge can produce a bigger and better reward. The disciple is no different. We must be willing to risk by "fishing deeper waters" for the bountiful harvest God has prepared, taking the risk that God's commands will produce His results, even when His commands don't make clear sense to us.

Fishermen are *optimists*. They believe in a positive future, that every cast will produce the next lake record or at least a bite. Disciples look to every relationship as being an opportunity to model God's love and grace with their fellow man. Modeling can be more of a challenge than simply telling someone about our Lord. As James reminds us, being a disciple includes being both a doer and a hearer of God's Word (James 1:22).

LINE AND NET SINKERS

A variety of stone sinkers to be used with hook and line or on nets

Fishermen methodically *prepare*. Rarely was a fisherman successful in Jesus' day, unless his equipment was in good shape. Nets had to be mended and cleaned, removing seaweed and other debris. Sinkers needed to be crafted and precisely hung on the nets. A first-century fisherman practiced throwing and retrieving his net to maximize his catch. A disciple is at his best when he is prepared to go fishing for souls. He prayerfully considers God's direction with an individual, asking the Holy Spirit to prepare the hearts of those who do not know Jesus. Effective followers study and absorb God's Word so that we can recall Scripture that is appropriate for the encounter.

Fishermen *catch* fish. Real fishermen aren't satisfied just flinging a fly or lure around. They see that the ultimate purpose of fishing is not just the sport of casting but actually catching fish. True disciples don't just fill a pew on Sunday, but are actively involved in "catching others for Christ" (see Matt. 4:19; Luke 5).

WHAT MAKES A GREAT FISHER OF MEN?

Casting a lure or fly is an art. One must know the characteristics of his equipment, the species of fish in the area, the water conditions, and many other facts about the environment and the surrounding elements. And so it is with men who want to "catch men." You must know the truth of the Word of God, the type of person with whom you are dealing, the background of the individual, and other pertinent information. For most of us, that means we need to recall essential verses of Scripture, utilize practical anecdotes that connect with the individual, and allow the Holy Spirit to work through us. Our responsibility is to be ready and prepared to speak a word of the hope that is within us (2 Tim. 2:15)—and thereby we proclaim the gospel of Jesus Christ. It is the work of the Holy Spirit to draw people to Christ. You and I don't "save" anyone—we are merely the guides who cast the line and then demonstrate with our lives the way of Christ (John 6:44).

In the back of the book is a section entitled "God's Game Plan for Life" that will acquaint you with one approach on how to use Scripture to present God's Word. In addition to knowing God's Word, the following concepts are to be applied:

* Develop an authentic relationship with a person. Others need to know that you really care about them and the things they care about.

* It is important to ask several questions to search out exactly where they are in their spiritual journey. Remember: listen, listen, listen.

✳ Find a common interest or hobby that can lead to informal times when both of you are relaxed and comfortable. A casual environment puts people at ease.

✳ Don't force the issue of uncomfortable conversations. Press gently into words and phrases that demonstrate compassion and interest. Don't be afraid of the silence in a conversation.

✳ People generally like to hear their names and to know you were listening. Each time you meet, recall things that were important to him (e.g., his work, his family, his interests).

✳ If the conversation or personality issues aren't working, then refer him to someone you think would better relate to him. If the relationship isn't happening, then don't push it.

✳ At the end of the day, it is about integrity. Mean what you say and say what you mean. If you promise something, make sure you follow up with what you say you will do.

✳ Be a good model—but when you mess up (we all do), then acknowledge your short-comings. If you're not transparent, you can't expect others to be.

✳ It is often through trials that people will be most open to consider a conversation on spiritual matters. Be sensitive to people who have lost their job or a loved one, who are going through a divorce or dealing with a troubled teen, and so forth.

✳ Unless the Holy Spirit leads you, don't try to "close the deal" too quickly. Leave him wanting more information.

A TRUE DISCIPLE

An angler teaches his trade to an apprentice one step at a time. Because there are so many variables in fishing, many repetitive sessions are often needed to thoroughly acquaint an angler with all the possible alternatives. Likewise, a disciple learns best by experiencing a teaching through custom or habit.

Picture of "Jesus Boat" from 1st century found in 1986 buried in the mud in the Sea of Galilee just a few miles from Peter's House in Capernaum.

Nineteenth-century biblical scholar J. H. Thayer suggested that "a *mathetes* is a special kind of learner—one who learns by use and practice."[2] I am sure that James must have realized this principle when he instructed his readers to prove themselves doers of the word rather than hearers who delude themselves (James 1:22).

A disciple is a "leader-in-training," a follower and believer. The disciple so identifies with the master's attitudes and actions that he becomes a leader himself. The process begins by receiving Christ as Lord and Savior and becoming a true believer and learner. A disciple is learning, growing, and preparing to teach others as he matures. True discipleship produces growth and evidence of maturity in wisdom and judgment. A disciple is a person-in-process who, through his lifestyle, consciously works to become more like Christ.

If we are sold out for Jesus and He is our passion, we will want to share our beliefs with others. Discipleship by its nature implies the idea of teaching and encouraging others in their faith. This happens because we make ourselves available and consider every opportunity as a time to build a bridge of understanding to the unsaved.

In the purest sense, discipling a person suggests that you are focused upon the spiritual development of an individual. Discipling a person is helping that person become Christlike in his motives, attitudes, and daily living. Pat Morley gave a good working definition of a disciple in his book *Pastoring Men*: "A disciple is someone *called* to live 'in' Christ, *equipped* to live 'like' Christ, and *sent* to live 'for' Christ."[3] Thus, a discipler is a person who will help equip the disciple to become more like Christ, so he in turn can disciple others.

As previously mentioned, I define a discipler or a spiritual mentor as someone who disciples others through relationships so as to fully connect with the person being mentored. Being a spiritual mentor is ultimately about building a relationship that can help both parties become stronger in their faith. If we agree that the most precious of gifts is *time*, then the idea of investing in others or having someone invest in you is a special gift. There will be things that you will have to sacrifice in order to focus on the most important thing— making disciples for Christ.

Mentoring and discipleship are very similar, and you will find that I use the terms interchangeably; however, the essence of finding *discipleship* is finding a spiritual mentor, who is willing to share the teachings of Christ as experienced in his life, with someone who genuinely desires to know God and make Him known. I like the term *spiritual mentoring* because it implies the heart of discipling another person within the context of a relational mentoring environment. That is to say, the most effective and long-lasting discipling relationships happen best when you seek to encourage and equip the person in areas beyond just the spiritual aspects of life. If you can find common interest areas such as sports, hobbies, cultural interests, work, or family, your relationship will have dimensions that will hold you together during trying times.

During the time of Christ, a spiritual teacher or mentor was called a *didaskalos* (Luke 2:46). Jewish teachers taught through the use of a discipleship process, allowing the students to ask questions to which the teacher would reply. They did not have any official position and received no salary. The person being discipled helped to support the discipler and meet his day-to-day needs. These teachers were common men who cared enough about others to share their lives and experiences to help others deal with life.

THE ULTIMATE FISHER OF MEN: ANDREW

No other disciple had more zeal and passion for the lost than Andrew. We first meet him in Scripture as he identifies himself as a follower and disciple of John the Baptist. Andrew and John were the first of the twelve to attach themselves to Jesus (John 1:35–40).

No sooner did Andrew discover Jesus for himself than he went to find his brother Peter to bring him to Jesus. Peter became acquainted with Jesus and became the undisputed leader of the apostolic band. Along with James and John, Peter formed an inner circle with their Savior, sharing some of His most intimate moments. Was Andrew envious or resentful? No way. Andrew was not worried about who was top dog. Disciples like him form the backbone of the Christian church and are the salt of the earth. On at least three separate occasions, Andrew emerges from the pages of John's Gospel as the consummate crusader concerned with evangelism (zealous effort to spread the gospel).

Andrew was constantly using his gifts, talents, fishing background, and personality to meet people in the marketplace of life and share his faith. He began by introducing his brother (Peter) to Jesus (John 1:40–42). On the second occasion, he brought to Jesus the lad with the five loaves and the two fish (John 6:8–9). Andrew was eager to bring anyone to Christ, even a little child. On the third occasion, we see Andrew doing the work of evangelism when he brings the Greeks to Jesus (John 12:20–22). The Greeks had come to Philip with the request to see Jesus, but Philip did not know what to do with them. After consulting with Andrew, he realized that he must take them to Jesus. As a professional fisherman, Andrew understood that no fish is too small or insignificant to bring ashore. He did not miss the opportunity of bringing anyone to Jesus who showed even the slightest interest in meeting his Master.

PRINCIPLES OF DISCIPLESHIP FROM ANDREW

Andrew understood Jesus so well that he knew his Master was never too busy to spend time with someone who was seriously seeking truth.

He is never too busy for you or me. He is always there to hear our prayers and provide the inspiration and guidance for our daily living.

Andrew's modeling of what it means to be a disciple presents some encouraging principles.

1. ANDREW SOUGHT TO BE UNSELFISH IN REPRESENTING CHRIST.

He knew that his brother Peter was a natural, instinctive leader. It didn't bother Andrew to take the backseat. There was no concern for who got the credit or why Christ favored others. Andrew was obedient to the call and sought to faithfully spread the word about the Savior. Often, this meant that Andrew gave up his own identity and recognition for the sake of honoring others. Later, tradition tells us that Andrew was a gifted communicator who preached in many lands. He obviously had the ability, but deliberately sought to serve Jesus and encourage others rather than to promote himself. Once he proved his faithfulness and loyalty, God gave him a powerful international ministry.

2. ANDREW WAS AN OPTIMIST.

Andrew saw the little boy with the five loaves and two fish as someone Jesus could use. It never occurred to Andrew that it was hopeless (John 6:8–9). He recognized that Jesus wished to use everyone. Andrew is said to have sought out the difficult areas to spread the Word. Places like Cappadocia, Bithynia, Galatia, and Byzantium were considered to be hostile lands filled with desperate people. Yet tradition has it that some of the disciples went to these lands with a sense of mission and purpose. Andrew's keen insights and optimistic heart greatly impacted these countries for Christ.

3. ANDREW WAS NOT PREJUDICED.

At a time when races and cultures did not mix with one another, Andrew sought to share God's Word with all people; he was universal in his outreach. Most Jews did not believe that another race could possibly be of any use to God. Gentiles were considered an accursed group of people. Andrew was the first of the disciples to realize that Christ's message was for all humanity. He crossed the racial and cultural barriers to present Christ as Lord and Savior to all.

LET'S GO FISHING

There is something about Andrew. He is like many of us. Life placed him in a position where he could have been resentful and embittered by being placed in a supportive role to Jesus and Peter, but he had a servant's heart about encouraging others in their giftedness and calling. The key thing is that Andrew always endeavored to glorify Christ and to bring people to Him.

Andrew was committed until the end. Tradition has it that he was scourged with rods by seven individuals, then fastened to an X-shaped cross and left to die. It was his wish not to die on the same type of cross as Jesus, for he felt unworthy. This was just another example of Andrew's humble spirit that consistently sought to glorify Christ.

He lived and died a true disciple and missionary. It is my aspiration, and hopefully yours, to imitate Andrew in my life. May we be allowed to die to self while engaged in the process of bringing others to Christ—and eternal life in Him. What a way to go!

FISHING FOR MEN

Spend time with your mentoring partner studying the following passages concerning Andrew, and consider what qualities Andrew had that make an effective fisher of men: John 1:40–42; 6:8–9; 12:20–22. What things would you need to do differently in your life to be more like Andrew? Share with each other how you see your mentoring partner stacking up against Andrew. What do you think your mentoring partner needs to work on? What do *you* need to work on?

THE **MASTER** FISHERMAN

FISHING TALE

My first recollection of fishing occurred when I was five years of age. My dad's family had an outing on the California Delta and, shortly after arriving at a beach area near Tracy, California, my grandma opened her picnic basket and began to put together lunch. The fishermen of the group baited up with chunks of smelly sardine and made their casts into the swift current. After a short period of time, they propped up their rods with some sticks and lined up for some of grandma's homemade ravioli and French bread.

At five years of age, I was more fascinated with the fishing than I was about eating. My dad placed his old stiff wooden rod and reel in my hands and said, "Son, watch this rod and reel and, whatever you do, don't let it go." No one had taught me a thing about fishing; therefore, whatever happened would just be out of instinct.

My focus was riveted on the point where the line entered the water, as I waited patiently for the slightest indication that something was happening. Then, without warning, the rod started jumping around in my hands. At first, I was startled and began to yell out for help. Then I realized that I needed to take control of the situation. The four-pound catfish at the end of that line had no idea that this event would fuel the fires of fascination and excitement that have lasted a lifetime.

Many people probably can't remember the details of their first date, first kiss, or first driving experience, but almost everyone can

Ancient heavy boat anchors found at the bottom of the Sea of Galilee

tell you *when, where,* and *how* they caught their first fish. Some say fishing is "a jerk on one end of a line waiting for a jerk on the other." I like to define the sport as "the art of casting, trolling, jigging, or spinning while freezing, sweating, swatting, or swearing." Fishing is definitely a sport that captures the imagination and passion of many people, and I'm often asked what it takes to become a successful fisherman.

First, there must be a decision. Tell yourself, "I want to be the best fisherman I can be." Making the decision is often the biggest hurdle. It involves counting the cost—the time, the effort, and the study required. After deciding to become a good fisherman, the next step is to seek out others who can help you apply the information, equipment, and resources you have acquired. You will want to carefully study the masters of the sport for information, techniques, and practical tips on the finer points of angling.

I was fortunate enough to be personally mentored by the best. Well-known national fishing pros like Al Lindner, Jimmy Houston, Hank Parker, Bill Norman, Stan Fagerstrom, Homer Circle, and many professional bass fishermen have assisted me in refining my skills and crafting my talents. I studied their approach, read their articles, and watched their video tapes until my approach to fishing so mimicked their style that many people wondered if I wasn't related to them. I fixed my *gaze* upon them so that their best traits and techniques would be lived out in my life. As these techniques and skills developed in my life and fishing career, I passed them on to others.

As I further identified with their style, knowledge, and experience, I became a student—a person focused upon the masters. I was not only able to fish with many of them but studied their videos, books, and articles. During my competitive fishing years and three years of filming fishing shows, I sought to fish with the masters at every opportunity. In so doing, I grew in my wisdom and understanding of fishing. But head knowledge will only take you so far. I've never known anyone to catch a fish from a couch. A real fisherman transfers that knowledge into his heart where it becomes a passion, a desire to take the knowledge and apply it into actual action.

An inspired angler decides to make life changes that will get him out to a stream or lake, where he can take his knowledge and practice his skills. It is when we are on the water that tying on a lure, casting, and cranking become a true extension of our mind and heart. The use of our rod, reel, and lure allows us to utilize our hands in accomplishing the task of catching a fish.

A FIRST-CENTURY APPROACH TO MENTORS

Modern-day fishing became popular because people were willing to communicate information and teach practical skills that lured people to advance fishing from a survival skill into one of the most popular leisure pursuits in the world. Even at the professional level, people embrace the joy of the sport within the context of the passion to conquer the wary denizens of the deep.

Christianity spread in part because the first-century disciples were consumed with the passion to know God and make Him known. As each disciple studied Jesus, the Master Fisherman, he was able to pass along information and experiences that could be used in the practical application of his faith to real-life situations.

FOLLOWING THE MASTER FISHERMAN

When Jesus said, "Follow Me, and I will make you fishers of men" (Matt. 4:19), He was beckoning all of us to bring our attitudes and actions into alignment with His Spirit. The "Follow Me" part of this verse is about a *head-level* decision with which a person seeks to know Christ through the leading of the Spirit. A disciple makes a decision to follow and know the living God. This happens by accepting who He is, what He did for our salvation, and why we need His comforting Spirit to live a life of significance.

To be a disciple also means that *head* knowledge of Christ moves toward the *heart.* If we truly desire to be like Him, then our knowledge must begin to translate into change from within. Our character, attitudes, behaviors, and priorities testify to this change through visible actions. The Holy Spirit transforms us into relational people who have a compassion for others. This becomes a *heart-oriented* transformation as we desire *to be like* Christ. We so identify with His teachings and character that we begin to mimic Him in our thoughts and actions (Eph. 5:1; 1 Thess. 1:6).

When we really know Christ and begin the process of a heart transformation, we will see how God wishes to use our hands. The ultimate purpose of the fisherman is to use his knowledge, desire, and hands to properly cast his rod, reel, and lure to a wary fish. When we become interested in fishing for men, the process must transfer into the hands through the heart and head. Most often, fishing for men involves using our hands and words through practical acts of service, works of kindness, spending time with others, and using our gifts, abilities, talents, and learned skills to develop relationships with others.

It has been said that people don't care about how much we know until they know how much we care. Think about it. If we want to build a relationship with another man, it most often begins with doing something together such as:

* mowing the neighbor's lawn when he is sick

* snowblowing an elder person's driveway

* helping a disabled person load his car after shopping

* inviting a lonely business associate over for a barbecue

* working with high-risk kids by taking them fishing, camping, or hiking

* seeking out those who are downtrodden to give them a word of inspiration

In the same way that I learned the sport of fishing, becoming a mature believer requires a willing spirit and some applied knowledge.

Willing and teachable spirit: A person must desire to expand his faith and seek out the truths that really transform a life. We must decide not to conform to the natural desires of our flesh, but to be transformed into a new person willing to be obedient to God's will for our lives. This starts with the *head knowledge* that God has ultimate power over His creation. Even the knowledge and rational thinking process is a gift of the Creator that separates us from the rest of His creation.

Practical application: Becoming a follower of Christ demands both a change of attitude and the practical application of the Holy Spirit leading us to revelations of God's plan for your life. We need to use our talents, experience, networks, influences, and skills to assist those who have needs.

Patience: Building intentional relationships isn't always pretty. There will be times when things get messy. There can be misunderstandings, doubt, distrust, disagreements, and times when your patience will be tested. Someone once said, "Anything worthwhile requires patience." When you are developing deep personal relationships with those you are mentoring, expect that there will be awkward moments. Satan will try to stand in the way of efforts to encourage someone in his faith. Don't let him have the victory; persevere!

WHO ARE YOUR SPIRITUAL MENTORS?

In the first century, an apprenticeship system was used to train people in a variety of tasks. That same approach was used with spiritual leaders. Those in training attached themselves to a rabbi and literally lived with him for a period of time. Their goal was both to learn all their teacher knew and to imitate his way of life. In the truest sense of the word, the apprentice became a student, a pupil or learner. Even though they were engaged in their jobs, families, and chores, apprentices took the time to be students of their master, just as the disciples did with Jesus. Faith was of major importance to the emerging church members. Sacrifice and perseverance were part of the cost they were willing to pay to know God and make Him known.

Only the wealthy fishermen could afford lead net weights like these.

I wonder if the church has made it too easy and too painless to be a follower of Christ. You rarely hear the word *sacrifice* in the modern church. I hear more about convenience, being seeker-sensitive, developing feel-good religion, and preaching cheap salvation than discussions about how we need to better integrate godly thinking into our daily living.

Each of us needs spiritually mature godly men who can speak into our lives. In our hectic world, it's hard to find men who are willing, equipped, and able to serve in that capacity—but it is worth the investment of our time to find men who will take seriously the role of a spiritual mentor. In my book *The Spiritual Mentor*, I go into more detail of defining terms and describing what a mentor looks like, but let's look at a short list of qualifications that could be considered when looking for your discipler:

* A man of God who follows Him in his daily living

* Someone who reads, absorbs, and seeks to live out God's Word in his life

* A person willing to spend an hour or two with you every week

* A man who is willing to be transparent and open—two qualities that are very important to living out abstract theology

* Someone who can be trusted with sensitive information

* An individual with relevant life experiences that connect with who you are

* Someone who enjoys activities that you can share beyond your study and discussion times together (golf, fishing, hunting, video games, woodworking, crafting, etc.)

* A man whose family reflects his dedication to being a good husband and father

* A person who has experienced some pain and suffering, so he can relate to your challenges

* Compassion that is balanced with firmness when it comes to accountability

Obviously, few mentors will have all these traits. This list could help you begin a search process that will connect you with a guy who can encourage your spiritual growth, while helping you focus on biblical truth.

WHAT MAKES A GREAT FISHER OF MEN?

When I think about focus and concentration, I am reminded how Jesus used an incident in the lives of His fisherman-disciples to help them remember where they needed to fix their *gaze*. Shortly after the miraculous feeding of five thousand people, the disciples left in their boat and found themselves in the midst of a storm. The disciples had left according to Jesus' instructions. We read in Matthew 14:22–23, "Immediately Jesus made His disciples get into the boat and go before Him to the other side, while He sent the multitudes away. And when He had sent the multitudes away, He went up on the mountain by Himself to pray. Now when evening came, He was alone there."

Jesus wanted to be alone to communicate with the Father and to rest from His demanding ministry. Of course, God does not need to rest, but Jesus, who is both God and man, needed to reenergize His body, mind, and spirit. He reclined on that gentle slope overlooking Tabgha Harbor on the northwest shore of the Sea of Galilee. The fishermen-disciples had already begun their evening work. The Sea of Galilee (also known as Lake Gennesaret, Lake Kinnereth, or the Sea of Tiberias) was a familiar location for the disciples. They knew that the best fishing with trammel nets (gill nets) came in the evening hours when the small bait fish came to the surface along the shoreline, bringing the bigger game fish with them.

These young men were still considering the call that Christ had made on their lives a few months earlier: "Follow Me, and I will make you fishers of men" (Matt. 4:19). They were still sorting through what it meant to be a disciple. Their faith was young and, like most accomplished fishermen, they were depending upon their own abilities and skills. We read in Matthew 14:24 that the disciples' boat was "in the middle of the sea, tossed by the waves, for the wind was contrary." This event took place "in the fourth watch of the night" (v. 25).

The disciples were having a tough time. The wind and waves had driven them many yards from shore, and the chill of the early morning hours was setting in. The "fourth watch" was from three to six o'clock in the morning when exhaustion hangs heavy and it seems it will never be daylight again. The imagination wanders and fear seems to grow. The dampness clings and bites. There were no comforting shoreline beacons in sight, and no lighted compasses aboard this old wooden boat. These tired fishermen were scared and disappointed. *Whose idea was this? Why didn't we stick with Jesus?* Their desperation may have drawn them into childish accusations. Then, at the point of their greatest concern, they saw Jesus.

But the disciples did not expect to encounter Jesus in this way. Verses 26–27 say, "And when the disciples saw Him walking on the sea, they were troubled, saying, 'It is a ghost!' And they cried out for fear. But immediately Jesus spoke to them, saying, 'Be of good cheer! It is I; do not be afraid.'"

In the original Greek, the word for *ghost* can be transliterated as "phantasm" or "phantom." The disciples thought they were seeing a ghost or a phantom spirit, but Jesus calmed the situation by announcing that it was He.

Peter was so impressed with this miracle that his immediate response was, "Lord, if it is You, command me to come to You on the water" (v. 28). Peter was a lot like many of us—impulsively direct! Many fishermen are short on patience and quick to take action without thoroughly considering all the factors involved. Peter wanted to step out in faith—he wanted to be with Jesus.

And Jesus said, "Come" (v. 29). Peter fixed his gaze upon the Lord and stepped onto the water. He did not walk around the boat or head off to a better fishing hole; he walked on water, and he walked straight toward Jesus. What happened to Peter next is the same thing that happens to all of us when we take our gaze off the Master—he sank. Peter broke contact with Jesus the moment his gaze became fixated on the wind—but how quickly he called out for help! Fortunately, the Lord was just as quick in His response, and He immediately reached out and grabbed him. In His love and faithfulness, Jesus was there for Peter, just as He is always there for us (Ps. 57:3).

Peter's mistake was that he allowed his concentration to wander away from Jesus and focus on the dangers around him. In the same way, a fisher of men needs to always keep his focus on Christ, even in the midst of danger or trials. The disciples were out on the water, engulfed in deep darkness, and they were frightened at the sight of what appeared to be a ghost walking on the water toward them. Rather than ask themselves why Jesus would send them into danger, they allowed their imaginations to run wild and became overcome with fear. The same thing can happen to us when unexpected challenges enter our lives. We forget that everything in our lives has been allowed by God, and we focus on the problems rather than on the faithfulness of God.

LIFE'S CHALLENGES:
OPPORTUNITIES TO TRUST GOD

Many of our daily tasks involve risk. Being a fisherman two thousand years ago was no easy task. The unfriendly elements and poor equipment posed challenges. Most of the fishing was done in the dark of the evening hours when the sea was most dangerous. Today, our equipment is better, but sometimes our judgment is lacking, and we still have to fight those unfriendly elements.

In life, we find continual challenges in our work environment, recreational activities, and family. We experience stress when we strive to order our private world and balance life's priorities. Many families are working through the backwash of brokenness and bitterness, trying to piece things together. All of us need to consider the challenges of life as opportunities to trust God.

We need to look for ways to expand our horizon. Like Peter, we need to step out in faith—even taking *a risk* based on our faith. We may sometimes find ourselves battering the winds of life, but there is always hope, no matter what we encounter. *God is with us.* Do you need to take a risk in developing a new friendship? Perhaps your risk is changing careers so you can enjoy more time with your family. Or maybe your risk involves trusting someone who has let you down. For most of us, it is important to consider who we can depend upon to be our spiritual mentor.

Risk requires that we recognize our inability to "go it alone"—*we need to trust the Lord.* We need the support of our Lord who can reach out and save us from the circumstances of life. Jesus says, "Take courage! It is I." God wants us to trust Him—to take courage.

LET'S GO FISHING

Peter had fixed his gaze upon Jesus. We might define *gaze* as a look that penetrates to the heart, a concentrated focus. Peter concentrated his focus on the Lord Jesus, and you and I need to do the same.

When we are truly focused upon our Lord with our prayer life, our worship, and our actions, *He Himself* handles our problems and conquers our fears. He makes us strong and able to walk boldly and with confidence (Prov. 3:26). How often we fail in maintaining our focus on Christ. The distractions and encumbrances of life surround us and we feel smothered. We need the Spirit of God who resuscitates us to life—*eternal* life. Psalm 27:4 states, "One thing I ask of the LORD, this is what I seek: that I may dwell in the house of the LORD all the days of my life, *to gaze upon the beauty of the Lord and to seek him in his temple*" (NIV, emphasis added).

David C. Needham, in his marvelous book *Close to His Majesty*, speaks of the great intimacy that results when we focus our gaze upon God:

> It is so easy to forget that God saved us above all else for love, for intimacy in relationship, for response. To fail to have time for this is to fail at living. Certainly His intentions are that everything

else—service, witnessing, practical holiness—be a byproduct of our love for Him. And nurturing love takes time. Where did we ever get the idea that it simply "happens?"[1]

In Proverbs 4:24–25, we find the counsel of the great King Solomon. Despite his wealth, wisdom, and fame, he reminds us of the most important thing—*keeping focused on God*: "Put away perversity from your mouth; keep corrupt talk far from your lips. Let your eyes look straight ahead, fix your gaze directly before you" (NIV). When distractions well up, seeking to draw our attention away from Christ, *that* is the most important time to keep our gaze—*our concentration*—focused solely upon Him. The author of Hebrews put it this way:

> Therefore, since we are surrounded by such a great cloud of witnesses, let us throw off everything that hinders and the sin that so easily entangles, and let us run with perseverance the race marked out for us. Let us fix our eyes on Jesus, the author and perfector of our faith, who for the joy set before him endured the cross, scorning its shame, and sat down at the right hand of the throne of God. (Heb. 12:1–2 NIV)

To be effective disciples, then, you and I must fix our eyes upon Jesus. As we keep our gaze focused on Him, all else in our lives will be seen in proper perspective. No problem seems too big—*for He is always with us.*

FISHING FOR MEN

Discuss with your mentoring partner some practical projects that you can do together this week to help someone in need, using the bulleted list in the appendix—then take the necessary steps to put those plans into action. As you think about an idea to help another person, what were the important moments in your life? Who influenced you the most? When did God come into your life to impact the decisions you are making?

THE **FORMULA** FOR **FISHING** **SUCCESS**

FISHING TALE

Anyone who would take fishing seriously can appreciate that, like any other sport, if you want to excel and be among the elite anglers, you need to develop a knowledge base that can be used to master the sport. Occasionally, you will hear about some young person fishing for trout in shallow water with a little salmon egg on four-pound test line with a superhero rod who hooks and lands a monster ten-pound bass. God has a sense of humor as He directs and allows these peculiar things to happen. But at the end of the day, the old adage is generally true that 10 percent of the fishermen catch 90 percent of the fish, and 90 percent of the fish are located in 10 percent of the ponds, lakes, or rivers.

During some work I did in Chattanooga back in the 1990s, I was often asked by organizations and businesses associated with fishing for advice on educating new people to fishing. Such was my pleasure in contributing a few ideas to some businessmen who were about to build one of the largest aquarium projects in the world. This aquarium would be unique, not only because of its design, but because of its emphasis on teaching people about fishing and some basic principles of limnology (study of water chemistry) and ichthyology (study of fish). Toward this end, the great Al Lindner and I joined forces to develop a fishing curriculum that could be used with this project and the associated National Fishing Center Project. (I realize that some people reading this book may wish to take up this crazy sport. In the following paragraphs, I will provide a brief explanation of the basic theory for being a successful fisherman before I share the biblical application.)

Al Lindner is a legendary television fishing show host and founder of the In-Fisherman Communications Network and *Angler's Edge* television program. He and his staff have developed some of the most progressive teaching methods to help educate people on how to become great fishermen. When I first met Al, I was teaching similar classes and programs at colleges and universities and during many sports shows. My "Fundamentals of Fishing" college classes in the late 1960s and early '70s were the nation's first accredited classes on fishing.

Al and I agree that most successful fishermen succeed precisely because they've been able to skillfully apply those basic principles received through study and observation. When aspiring anglers take the time to study specific teachings that can assist them with their favorite pursuit, they tend to remember and apply the correct strategy at the appropriate time. We become better at what we do because we intentionally find ways to remember things that work or make us better. Today we have compact video cameras, recorders, and other electronic hardware that we can take along on our excursions to record our thoughts and actions so we can review them at a later date.

Using technology and social media, it is pretty easy for someone to put together a log of his fishing experiences. By researching and cataloging the best of the literature, experiences, and advice available, you can develop some kind of an instruction manual or journal that helps you remember the important points and applications. Contained within the pages of my personal "Fishing Instruction Manual" is the formula for fishing success that Al and I used for years. The basic formula is this: F + L + P = Fishing Success.

F + L + P = FISHING SUCCESS

We need to really know about the distinguishing features of the *fish* (F) that we are pursuing. Each fish hangs out in a different *location* (L) and seeks out the company of its own kind. How we *present* (P) the lure to the fish is key to the *success* of catching that fish. Learning to fish can be broken down into a simple recipe that will help eliminate those "empty creel days." This formula can be used for either freshwater or saltwater species. The formula was used by first-century fishermen, and it is still used by tournament pros today.

F: FISH FACTOR

Before you bait a hook, you'd better understand the nature of the fish you're attempting to catch. Each species of fish has its own peculiar habits and behavior. Each species responds differently to its environment and to the offerings of a fisherman. Responses to your efforts hinge largely on the particular fish's sense of smell, taste, sight, touch, and hearing. The individual anatomy of the fish provides a clue to its limitations and abilities. For example, barracuda and salmon, with their sleek bodies, were designed by God to be swift in movement with enormous endurance. The catfish, in contrast, has a flat, wide body that is not conducive to speed but is suited for hugging the bottom while looking for food.

Similarly, sturgeons and sharks have a great sense of smell because of how God created their olfactory glands (smelling organ). The bluegill, in contrast, has a less developed olfactory system, thereby limiting its reliance on smell as a way to survive. Moreover, each species of fish has its own preferred temperature and oxygen range, food source (forage), and seasonal reproduction process. The more we understand about the "Fish Factor," the better judgments we will make about bait selection and areas to fish.

L: LOCATION FACTOR

Any good fisherman (or real-estate agent) can tell you that there are three fundamentally important things one must always remember:

location, *location*, and *location*. Knowing where to look for those sought-after "honey holes" where schools of fish congregate is a pivotal key to fishing success. Certain fish, such as black bass, crappie, or bluegill, typically hang out around warm water near brush piles, logs, piers, pilings, tulles, rocks, and grass beds. Those of us in the fishing industry call this stuff "structure."

In a lake setting, fish such as trout, salmon, and stripers typically cruise about in those open-water areas that are well oxygenated with cooler temperatures. Knowing whether the creature is an "open-water feeder" or a "close-to-structure" fish is important in seeking out the proper area in which to fish.

Once again, temperature, oxygen, light penetration, topography, and seasons play an important role in understanding the preferences of a fish on a given day. Even the barometric pressure can have a dynamic effect on the locational patterns of fish.

P: PRESENTATION FACTOR

Presentation refers to the actual process of presenting our bait or lure to the fish. Tackle selection, casting, lure placement, proper use of electronics, and boat placement are all part of the process. Proper presentation requires constant study, investigation, and practice. If a person understands the first two of these factors and fails to *apply* his knowledge correctly, he will fail to become a good fisherman. These factors represent the basic building blocks needed to be an effective angler. Patience, perseverance, and concentration cannot be applied if you do not first build the proper foundation.

JESUS' FISHING TECHNIQUES

Like a skilled fisherman, Jesus recognized the importance of building strength and character into His disciples. He asked that each disciple commit totally and wholeheartedly to the principles that would form the superstructure for true discipleship. He knew His disciples well. He had seen them study their fishing trade and apply selected strategies to various situations. Now it was time to transfer those techniques to something far more important than a load of fish. *It was time to go fishing for souls.* It was critically important that Jesus' disciples understand His instructions on how to be fishers of men, as they would need to practice good "fishing technique" after He ascended to heaven. It was through the inspiration of the Holy Spirit that Matthew recorded his Master's words to produce what I call Jesus' Instruction Manual of Discipleship.

In Matthew 9:9, the final disciple, Matthew, is selected. By now, most of the disciples had been with Christ for some time, and had witnessed His many miracles and listened to His teaching. As the Master Teacher, Jesus imparted knowledge that would be used to change the world. Much like teaching someone to become a great angler, Jesus used a systematic and direct approach to His followers. His building blocks for ministry were clearly set forth as an Instruction Manual of Discipleship that is still being used today to bring people into relationship with God.

THE KINGSHIP OF CHRIST

Matthew's Gospel affirms the kingship of Christ. Implied in his affirmation is a call for people everywhere to submit to that kingship. In Matthew 10:2–4, we meet the twelve men who had openly proclaimed, "Christ is our King." They had sacrificed everything to be His disciples. They gave up their careers and their lifestyles to submit to His authority. Throughout the first half of Matthew 10, we find Jesus directing His disciples and giving them "power and authority" for ministry. He instructs them on their immediate mission with respect to where they should stay and what they should do. He warns them that they, like all who would work in the Lord's name, will be persecuted and will come to understand the importance of sacrifice.

Jesus recognized that we can't live our lives alone. There are too many temptations, too many distractions; we become self-absorbed and fearful. Not only do we need the power of the Holy Spirit to guide us, but we also need a companion to help us and hold us accountable. Jesus sent His men out in pairs so that they could support and encourage one another. With someone else involved, you have built-in accountability and it doubles your efforts to impact others.

WHAT MAKES A GREAT FISHER OF MEN?

In Matthew 10:24–42, Jesus gives His disciples six principles or building blocks to be recorded in their "Instruction Manuals," so they will be properly equipped to meet the challenges before them. While some of His instructions are given explicitly to the twelve disciples, we see in verse 23 that Jesus talks to *future* disciples by suggesting that we should work until "the Son of Man comes." His clear word on discipleship was directed to anyone calling himself a believer. What was relevant in the first century is still relevant today.

LET'S GO FISHING!

1. BE LIKE ME (MATT. 10:24)

The first part of the "fishing for men" process involves the fish themselves, and the most important element of this phase is for each of us to become like Christ. "A disciple is not above his teacher, nor a servant above his master." We live in a culture today where we constantly hear the message, "it's all about me." Over and over again, we hear that we need to be our own person, be unique, stand out. But Christ calls us not so much to be our own person as to be *His* person, recognizing that modeling Christ is the best we can be. It is enough for the disciple to be like his teacher and the servant like his master (Matt. 10:24). That is the bedrock of discipleship. We are to be like our teacher, our master, our Lord, our King.

Remember, a disciple is a leader-in-training—a *learner*. And to the degree humanly possible we are to have *His* values, priorities, attitudes, compassion, and loving spirit. The topic of discipleship, of spiritual mentoring, is found throughout Christ's teaching because

He desires people to count the cost of following Him. Doing so is fundamental to our faith. Jesus is perpetually involved in perfecting the saints for the work of ministry—and He uses us in the process. You and I as disciples are to make *other* disciples who can, in turn, reproduce themselves. All the various aspects of Christ's ministry were directed to maturing His disciples for service. If we are true believers, we should be maturing in *our* faith while encouraging others to mature in *their* faith.

In James 1:22–25, Christ's disciples are reminded that they must be doers of the Word, not just hearers. Remember, more people will come to Christ by your *modeling* than by your *words*. It is good to focus upon the fact that we don't need to *speak* the message; we *are* the message. To paraphrase St. Francis of Assisi, "Always testify of Jesus; when necessary, use words."

A primary ministry of the Holy Spirit is to help us *to be*, not merely *to do*. Scripture tells us, "But you shall receive power when the Holy Spirit has come upon you; and you shall be witnesses to *Me* in Jerusalem, and in all Judea and Samaria, and to the end of the earth" (Acts 1:8, emphasis added).

Are you more worried about *doing* than *being*? Do your efforts sometimes seem fruitless? Maybe you are more concerned about the *look* of ministry than its *function*. The Great Commission is often misinterpreted with an emphasis placed upon *the doing*. The primary focus of this commission is upon *making disciples*, not "going," "baptizing," or "teaching." These things are merely the by-products of our discipling efforts.

I think many of us spend too much time wondering what we can do for Jesus rather than what He can do through our yielded lives. Jesus constantly reminds us that our daily walk is our testimony.

Luke 6:40 provides further encouragement to this point: "A student is not above his teacher, but everyone who is fully trained *will be like his teacher*" (NIV, emphasis added). The spiritual barometer against which we must continually measure ourselves is encapsulated in this statement: *you say you follow Christ; then show me your Christlikeness.*

When I focus upon the character of God and the teachings of Christ, *that* is when I mature in my faith. It really is not important what I think of myself, or what others might think, or how I believe others may see me. What *is* important to understand is how God sees me and how I can better emulate Him in my daily walk.

2. DO NOT BE AFRAID OF THE WORLD (MATT. 10:25–31)

The second element of being good fishers of men involves *location*. Our location is primarily this world; as Jesus taught, the world itself is our mission field (Matt. 13:38; 24:14). Yet this fallen world in which we live can be a frightening place. Three times in Matthew 10, Jesus instructed His disciples not to be afraid, repeatedly telling His disciples "do not fear."

Jesus tried to calm the disciples' fears because they had just heard Him describe a series of troubles they would encounter:

* They would be sent out as sheep in the midst of wolves (v. 16).

* They would be scourged in the synagogues (v. 17).

* They would be brought before governors and kings for His sake (v. 18).

* They would be arrested (v. 19).

* Their own families would cause them to be put to death (v. 21).

* They would be hated by all for His name's sake (v. 22).

* They would be persecuted for their beliefs (v. 23).

The fear of men can strangle the effectiveness of our ministry. If we become mere men-pleasers, we will give up on the ideals of our faith. There will be the constant temptation to pull back on our testimony and not be confrontational or defensive when the situation dictates.

Left: Section of reconstruction in the National Maritime Museum, Haifa
Right: Stone anchor on prow of Egyptian boat. From bas-relief in tomb,
ca. 3000 BCE

If we are like Christ, we will be treated like Him. The world treated Christ like the Devil (Beelzebub): "If they have called the master of the house Beelzebub, how much more will they call those of his household!" (Matt. 10:25). I think many of us are afraid to go into the world with our faith because of what others might think of our love for the Lord. Anyone can model Christlikeness in the confines of a loving church or Christian camp environment. But the real test comes when we are out in the world among those who don't like Jesus and dislike our allegiance to Him.

Jesus tells us that there will be a day when everything will be made right. God will make the truth known. He will reward and vindicate His own. We need to maintain an eternal perspective. When fishing for fish, we need to keep in mind what locations will be suitable for what we're after. If we lose our strategic perspective, we won't catch any fish. When fishing for men, we must keep in mind that the location where men are found is a fallen world. If we are worried about being popular or wise or noble in today's society instead of confronting an evil world, we've lost our eternal perspective.

I remember sitting in a pastor friend's office after a wonderful lunch and great fellowship when he offered some wise counsel from God's Word. I had been lamenting over my failure to please a few board members, and my friend had me read Galatians 1:10, which states, "For do I now persuade men, or God? Or do I seek to please men? For if I still pleased men, I would not be a bondservant of Christ."

Whose praise are you seeking? Remember that the praise of men can be fickle. We need to proclaim our allegiance to Christ and "preach on the housetops" (Matt. 10:27). Without being obnoxious, we should go into the world, leaving the security of our churches, and proclaim Him to be the King of kings and Lord of lords. We shouldn't alter our message and lifestyle for fear of what other people's reactions might be. The apostle Paul certainly didn't worry about those who threatened to throw him in jail.

Discipleship involves an identification with Christ in His victories *and* His rejection. Paul had it figured out: "That I may know Him and the power of His resurrection, and the fellowship of His sufferings, being conformed to His death" (Phil. 3:10).

3. PUBLICLY CONFESS JESUS AS LORD (MATT. 10:32–33)

The third element in successful fishing involves *presentation*, the art of presenting our lure or bait to the fish in an attractive way that will compel the fish to bite. When fishing for men, the same principle holds true: we must learn how to present the truth of Christ in a compelling way. I am not suggesting that we need to make the gospel "relevant" to current fads and fashions. On the contrary, a successful fisher of men does not present the *gospel*; he presents *Christ*.

Jesus told His disciples, "Therefore whoever confesses Me before men, him I will also confess before My Father who is in heaven" (Matt. 10:32). We must be willing to agree, affirm, and confess that Jesus is Lord. If we believe our faith should be kept a secret, we have missed the purpose of discipleship. We need to be genuine in our commitment. We demonstrate that authentic commitment by openly proclaiming His presence in our lives.

Once again, the apostle Paul helps us understand this concept with his challenge to the early disciples in Rome: "If you confess with your mouth the Lord Jesus and believe in your heart that God has raised Him from the dead, you will be saved" (Rom. 10:9). A true disciple confesses his faith before men. Jesus then affirms His loyalty to us by acknowledging before our heavenly Father that we are His children, washed in the cleansing blood of the Lamb. If we persist in denying our allegiance to Christ, however, then on the day of judgment Jesus will disown us: "But whoever denies Me before men, him I will also deny before My Father who is in heaven" (Matt. 10:33).

We can deny our faith in numerous ways. Our unchristian actions and attitudes can deny Him. Keeping silent when a testimony is called for can deny Him. Our lack of encouragement to a struggling brother or sister in the Lord can be a point of denial. If we sense a conviction of the Holy Spirit when we have failed in this respect, then we need to rethink our response so we won't fail the next time around. To be sure, we have *all* failed in many areas. By our nature, we all have lapses. If we are repentant and have a sense of brokenness regarding our lapse, then we have the heart of a believer. We can ask God for His grace and move on to live a more Christlike life. I'm embarrassed to count the number of times God provided the perfect opportunity for me to share my faith, but in my silence I denied Him. Thankfully, as I have matured in the Lord, those times have become fewer and fewer. Are you finding it more comfortable to be a witness?

4. YOUR COMMITMENT TO DISCIPLESHIP MAY CAUSE DIVISION

Jesus said, "Do not think that I came to bring peace on earth. I did not come to bring peace but a sword" (Matt. 10:34). This is paradoxical to our understanding. Jesus is the "Prince of Peace," yet His presence in our lives will split and fracture some of our relationships.

There is peace in the one who believes, but to the one who doesn't know Him there will be alienation and rejection. The sword of conviction and dedication will split many relationships. The extreme example of this division can be seen in the context of a home. Your commitment to Jesus Christ may need to go against the love and harmony of your household. It doesn't have to be that way, but if it comes to holding on to truth and your commitment to discipleship, then one must bear the pain of a divided home. Jesus warned His disciples that He had come to earth knowing full well that He would cause division, even within a person's own household.

Sometimes rejection can come from friends. I remember well the time when Louise and I decided to make Jesus the Lord of our lives. We worried about the reaction from friends and family. Many of our closest friends and some family members no longer involved us in many of their activities. For a time we felt so alone and dejected. Then we became involved in a local community church and found that God replaced broken relationships with new friends who could be counted upon during the tough times.

There is one thing even more precious than our relationship with friends or family members: *the love of our own life.* Jesus took His disciples one step further in testing their commitment and dedication: "And he who does not take his cross and follow after Me is not worthy of Me. He who finds his life will lose it, and he who loses his life for My sake will find it" (Matt. 10:38–39).

The disciples at this point had not heard about Calvary's cross, so what is the cross that Jesus wanted His disciples to take up? The disciples realized He was talking about dying. They were aware of the likelihood that either the Romans or the Jews would ultimately kill them for their passion and beliefs.

A mark of genuineness for a true disciple, then, is the forsaking of self, even to the point of death. Today we do not have Roman soldiers persecuting us or dens of lions to face. For most people in the United States, standing up for personal faith is not a threatening thing. But what if it *were* a life-threatening issue? What if a foreign power suddenly invaded America and all Christians were commanded to leave their faith or die? According to the book of Revelation, one day you may have to make that choice. *How will you choose?*

If confronted with this dilemma, are we willing to die for Christ's sake? If not, Jesus' teaching is quite clear. If, however, we are willing to pick up our cross and follow Him, we will see the blessings of ministry. The positive eternal rewards of our faith are clear. There are some things that are "all or nothing." Discipleship is one of those things.

5. RECEIVE THE REWARDS OF MINISTRY

Every disciple faces the potential for division and persecution. However, there exists an even greater potential that God could use you for expanding His kingdom. Jesus told His disciples, "He who receives you receives Me, and he who receives Me receives Him who sent Me" (Matt. 10:40). If we are striving to be like Him, then when someone receives us, *they receive the Lord.*

Jesus also told the disciples, "He who receives a prophet in the name of a prophet shall receive a prophet's reward. And he who receives a righteous man in the name of a righteous man shall receive a righteous man's reward" (v. 41). A disciple's character is manifested in his speaking (as a prophet) and living (as a righteous man), and this becomes a source of testimony to the world in which we live. Even the small acts of kindness to "the little ones"—people young in the faith—will be rewarded by our Lord.

A disciple in part determines the destiny for those with whom he comes into contact. He is the hook that God can use to fish the ponds of life, periodically catching a soul. As His disciples, we need to evaluate the depth of our commitment in light of His "Instruction Manual." Are we willing to identify with Him without fear, while publicly confessing and submitting to the point of forsaking family or even losing our own lives? That is what Jesus asked His first-century disciples to do. *This is what He asks of us today.*

6. EXPECT INCREASING LEVELS OF SACRIFICE

Did you notice the increasing levels of sacrifice in Matthew 10 that our Lord demanded of His followers in order to be a committed disciple? Are you willing to follow Him wholeheartedly? During many of the pastor training workshops that Men's Ministry Catalyst puts on, I ask pastors three questions to determine if they are really interested in church growth or in developing a culture of discipleship:

✳ Are you a committed disciple as defined through God's Word?

✳ Are you presently mentoring a group of men?

✳ Are you committed to leading a church that makes discipleship and mentoring a top priority?

If the pastors can't answer with an affirming "yes" to all the above, then I suggest to them that they may want to reconsider what God is doing in their lives and ministry. I like what the apostle Paul said: "Know His will, and approve the things that are excellent, being instructed out of the law, and are confident that you yourself are a guide to the blind, a light to those who are in darkness, an instructor of the foolish, a teacher of babes, having the form of knowledge and truth in the law" (Rom. 2:18–20). This, my friend, is what makes a great spiritual mentor.

FISHING FOR MEN

With your mentoring partner, carefully consider the fishing formula of fish, location, and presentation $(F + L + P)$ as it relates to fishing for men. How did Jesus and the disciples put this formula into practice? In practical terms, how will you put it into practice this week? As you meet with your mentoring partner, process the six building blocks mentioned in this chapter. What do they mean to you? What struggles have you experienced that have been most difficult and how did you handle them? How could you have better appropriated God's Word into problem-solving the issues?

ARE **YOU** **EQUIPPED** TO **GO FISHING?**

FISHING TALE

Imagine what it was like to be a Galilean fisherman during the time of Christ. After a short night's sleep, you wake up only to see the little oil lamp in your underground shelter flickering in the cold evening air. You gather your personal belongings and a tunic to help warm your body as you step outside to welcome your fishing companions.

The previous afternoon, you had packed your boat with several different types of nets, a couple of oars, and a few snacks to energize you for the physical task of pulling loaded nets full of fish into your boat. As you push off from shore, one of the four guys in the boat lights a polished brass pan that hangs out over the water. The reflection from the pan provides the only nearby light source onto the water. The stars overhead provide a guidance system so you can locate the spot on the water where you last caught fish.

The small sail is raised, and you coast away from the shore into the dark eerie shadows. The noise of the waves against the hull and the idle chatter of your weary friends are the only things that break through the chill of the night air. As soon as you reach your spot, the order is given to release and the front and rear stone anchors are thrown overboard. As the slack in the rope is taken up, the twenty-three-foot boat comes to rest in the perfect spot. The nets are once again checked before they are deployed. A prayer for a good catch is murmured by all as the fishermen cast the soggy nets into the dark water.

A first-century fisherman had to be sure all his equipment was in proper condition. The nets needed to be mended. The proper stone weights were spaced perfectly on the edges of the nets. The paddles were needed to adjust their position on the water. The rope and anchors were crafted in such a way that they did their job without a hitch. The single sail always needed attention due to the strain of the wind on the mast. Having the right equipment was a must for any ancient fisherman.

HAVING THE RIGHT EQUIPMENT

Today a good fisherman still relies on having the appropriate equipment to do his job. In preparing for a day's fishing, a master fisherman thoughtfully selects the necessary equipment for his trip. Careful attention is given to details. Only equipment that is clean and operating efficiently will be selected. This minimizes the potential for disruption or frustration due to equipment failure.

The most important equipment a modern-day fisherman needs are his rod and reel, the fishing line, and a good assortment of tackle. Without these basic tools, he would find fishing very frustrating, if not impossible. Just as a fisherman needs the right equipment to fish, so a disciple must have the right resources for the specific task God has set before him. In what follows and in keeping with the fishing theme, we will draw some analogies between the fisherman's equipment and that used by the disciple.

ROD AND REEL: SPIRITUAL GIFTS AND NATURAL TALENTS

The rod and reel are very important to the success of a fisherman. The make or quality of the gear is not nearly as important as knowing how to use each item effectively. A rod must be sensitive enough to feel the light bite of a timid fish, while sturdy enough in the butt section to set the hook into the jaw of the fish. Selection of a rod should be based on the species that one is attempting to catch, and the type of fishing that one wishes to pursue.

My favorite way to catch a fish is by using an ultra-light rod with a fast taper action that enables me to have both the needed sensitivity *and* the strength to work effectively. Despite the size, though, the most important thing is that the rod and reel be properly balanced with the line, lures, and angler's level of competence.

Just as there are different types of rod and reel combinations, so there are a variety of spiritual gifts. "There are diversities of gifts, but the same Spirit," the apostle Paul tells us (1 Cor. 12:4). Each of us "having then gifts differing according to the grace that is given to us, let us use them: if prophecy, let us prophesy in proportion to our faith" (Rom. 12:6). These gifts include serving, teaching, encouraging, contributing to the needs of others, leadership, and showing mercy (Rom. 12:6–8). Other gifts are listed in 1 Corinthians 12:1–11.

We need *all* the spiritual gifts working in harmony in order to function as an effective body of believers. Our gifts are to be used as functioning equipment that can enable the Holy Spirit to work within and through us. Regardless of what spiritual gifts we may have, *all* our gifts are to be used in honoring and serving our Lord. As the apostle Peter put it, "As each one has received a gift, minister it to one another, as good stewards of the manifold grace of God" (1 Peter 4:10).

If we are to be truly effective disciples, we must meet people in the marketplace of life and use our spiritual gifts *and* our talents to share the greatest news of all—*salvation in Jesus Christ.*

FISHING LINE: THE HOLY SPIRIT

It is imperative that a master fisherman continually check and restore his fishing line. The line is the vital link between the rod and reel and the lures. There are a variety of lines, and the quality varies with the cost of the product. It is important to always have enough good

Trammel net boat, 19th century drawing

line on your reel to provide the best possible chance of catching that fish of a lifetime.

Most major manufacturers produce fishing lines that are abrasive-resistant and minimize line stretch. These are important factors that affect the setting action on the fish. Line should be frequently checked and replaced—particularly after heavy use or fishing around abrasive objects such as trees, rocks, and brush.

As a fisherman depends on good line, so a disciple depends on the Holy Spirit. A disciple must constantly walk in dependence upon the Holy Spirit for guidance, direction, and wisdom (Gal. 5:16). The Holy Spirit is a divine enabler who empowers us to use our gifts (rods and reels) and testimonies (lures) effectively as we relate with others.

John the Baptist prophesied that Jesus would come and baptize with the Holy Spirit (Luke 3:16). This was ultimately fulfilled on the day of Pentecost (Acts 2). Since that time, every believer experiences the baptism of the Holy Spirit (1 Cor. 12:13). Prior to sending out

His disciples, Christ spoke of the importance of the Holy Spirit as an encourager and teacher: "But the Helper, the Holy Spirit, whom the Father will send in My name, He will teach you all things, and bring to your remembrance all things that I said to you" (John 14:26).

A disciple-fisherman needs to be filled with the Holy Spirit (Eph. 5:18). The daily challenges of life are sometimes abrasive and demanding and, through ministering to others, we periodically empty our spool of resources and need to be filled with the Spirit so that we can continue to serve our Lord. Our lives cannot be sustained without renewal from God. It is essential to replace the body's energy by eating, sleeping, good nutrients, and exercising. Similarly, the Christian cannot function without his soul being revitalized by reading God's Word (as illuminated by the Holy Spirit), listening to Spirit-filled Bible teaching, and by participating in the soul-filling table of Communion. The prophet Isaiah urged, "And let the people renew their strength! Let them come near, then let them speak" (Isa. 41:1).

Part of revitalizing our lives involves taking time to be still and listen to God (Ps. 46:10). In humble prayer, draw near to the footstool of His divine mercy, and realize the fulfillment of His promise: "But those who wait on the LORD shall renew their strength" (Isa. 40:31). He will always hold us as the object of His infinite affection and encouragement.

THE TACKLE BOX AND THE LURES: OUR TESTIMONIES AND LIFE EXPERIENCES

A good fisherman will have different baits and lures that can be used to catch a variety of fish in different situations. Each fisherman has his favorite lures and will most effectively use them when fishing gets difficult. Each lure has a purpose and can be selected according to its particular effectiveness.

We might liken the tackle box and assorted lures to our personal testimonies. Those intimate, life-changing experiences and memories help equip us to share with others the personal relationship we enjoy with the Lord. Just as good bait attracts a fish, so we can attract unbelievers to the Lord by our vibrant testimonies. Each day brings new opportunities for the Lord to do His miracles and to build memories in our lives that will encourage us and others in our spiritual journeys. Life's experiences provide unique snapshots that can be shared with others. Truly there is power in a vibrant testimony (Rev. 12:11).

WHAT MAKES A GREAT FISHER OF MEN?

Upon Christ's resurrection and appearance to the eleven disciples, He issued the Great Commission to them along the same shoreline where He first met them. He said, "All authority has been given to Me in heaven and on earth. Go therefore and make disciples of all the nations, baptizing them in the name of the Father and of the Son and of the Holy Spirit, teaching them to observe all things that I have commanded you; and lo, I am with you always, even to the end of the age" (Matt. 28:18–20). I am sure most Christians have heard or read the Great Commission many times. Yet, it is surprising how many of us are still standing on the shore, watching others fish. Perhaps some feel their equipment is not good enough? Have we forgotten who issues the equipment?

Many believe this work should be left to the real pros—pastors, priests, missionaries, and church workers. But the Great Commission was written to *all* Christians. James reminds us, "But be doers of the word, and not hearers only, deceiving yourselves" (James 1:22). If we are going to be "doers" of the Word, we must participate in fulfilling the Great Commission. Of course, there are some who feel that the fish, the lost souls, might not be interested. However, God promises that His Word will not return to Him void (Isa. 55:10–11).

A disciple serious about his call realizes that there exists a God-shaped vacuum in every man's heart that only Jesus can fill. People are seeking meaning and purpose in life. The reality is that the "fish" are very hungry. Our concern, then, is more a question of *how* and *when* we present the Word in a way they can understand.

In his book *Jesus Christ, Disciplemaker*, Bill Hull suggested, "When Jesus calls a person, he calls him or her to a purpose, a dream, a goal, a life-changing vision. The vision is to be a fisher of men. These Galilean men [the disciples] understood fishing, and they were certainly acquainted with the lost state of men. Therefore, the call to fish for men turned their heads; their hearts were aflame with the idea!"[1]

When you stop and think about it, there are people you see every day who will never see Jesus in anyone but you. They may have never entered a church, gone to a Bible study, or watched an evangelistic television program. That is why we need to understand the importance of using our gifts and talents to be fishers of men.

LET'S GO FISHING

How have you prepared your heart and spirit to serve the Lord (Ps. 51:10)? Think about this list and pray that God might encourage you to be that witness:

* I've embraced what it means to be an effective disciple (fisher of men) of Jesus.

* I will seek opportunities to enrich my life with God's wisdom and Word.

* My pastor and men's leader will be made aware of my desire to serve and utilize my gifts.

* It will be important to think about the choices I'm making in the things I put into my head.

* I will let my actions testify to what is in my spirit.

Most Christians I know have never biblically analyzed their spiritual gifts. Here are some suggestions on how to determine your spiritual gifts and talents.

✳ Go online or get a book on how to identify your spiritual gifts.

✳ Ask your pastor or a mature believer to assist you in determining your purpose and gifts.

✳ What comes natural to you? Most often your gifts are found in the things that you love to do.

✳ Ask your family and friends to tell you what particular thing you do exceptionally well and that blesses them most.

FISHING FOR MEN

Meet with your mentor and ask him to give you some guidance on evaluating how effective you have been in using the gifts, talents, and experiences God has given you. Don't give up hope. Everyone is needed in kingdom work.

What unique testimonies and experiences has God given you to share with others? Every person, no matter their background, has a story to tell. Maybe you had a close call with death or some trip that was unique or someone who blessed you; maybe you went through a divorce or God provided a miracle. It matters not the story if God was in it. Share it with others as a way to connect with their lives. People won't care what you have to say until they know how much you care.

How is fishing for men similar to fishing for fish? Are you presenting the message in a way that doesn't frighten the unsaved person? When sharing a specific story isn't connecting with the person, have you tried another approach? One difference between fishing for fish and fishing for souls is that it's God's responsibility to clean them. The messy part of the job comes when we try to be another man's god. Our responsibility is to be the man's spiritual mentor. We are to reflect light into darkness (Rom. 2:18–20).

DON'T GET **LOST**

FISHING TALE

Have you ever been lost? It can be a scary feeling, particularly if you are in a potentially hostile environment without anyone around to help you find your way. The feelings of helplessness, isolation, and uncertainty can grip your soul. Your heart begins to pound, as you realize that you might be lost, abandoned, and for-gotten. Sweat beads up on your forehead, as you try to remember which way to go. Your soul cries out: "I want my daddy!"

It is particularly challenging to keep a good orientation when you are in unfamiliar areas, fog on a lake or ocean, heavily forested lands, desolate prairies, or snow-laden territories. These can challenge your sanity. I remember the fear that overwhelmed me when I got lost in a department store at the age of five. Then when I was eleven, I went to an unfamiliar store for an ice cream a few blocks from my uncle's shop and got lost trying to get back. I think those early childhood traumas etched into my mind the importance of knowing where you are, where you are going, and how to rely on someone with a better perspective than yours.

For most people, whenever our lives are in danger and we sense a loss of control, we find that fear can grip our emotions and choke out any sense of logic and calmness. Such was the case of the fisher-men-disciples on at least two reported accounts in the Bible: Mark 6:45–51, rowing across the Sea of Galilee; and Matthew 8:24–27, when Jesus was asleep in the boat during a gale.

As we read these two stories, it is interesting to note that these seasoned fishermen and boaters became very anxious and confused as they endeavored to fight for their lives. For many of us, there are times when we are unsettled and stress filled as we endeavor to find a way forward from our present problem or uncomfortable circumstances. Fear has a way of challenging our common sense and abiding faith. It can strangle our sense of purpose and put a temporary blanket over our hope for the future. And remember, these guys out on that lake in Galilee were experienced fishermen who had seen storms before. The storms they experienced on these two occasions must have been special and different in some way for them to have been so frightened.

SO YOU'RE LOST—NOW WHAT?

It might have helped our first-century fishermen if they would have thought about one of the basic axioms that has saved many lost souls, whether on land or sea. *Stop!* is an easy word to remember that can translate into a message of hope for those people feeling lost.

Think about it. If you get lost, that is not the time for panic. A lost person needs to think: Right now, you're in no danger. You may not know exactly where you are, but misplacing yourself is only a problem if you allow it to become one. It is nothing to be embarrassed about; even the most experienced boater, fisherman, hiker, or woodsman has found himself disoriented on occasion. The difference is that he knows it is not a serious problem yet, and it won't become one because he is prepared with knowledge and some basic tools. I like the S.T.O.P. acronym developed by Douglas S. Ritter of the Equipped to Survive Foundation, as it can be very helpful if you should find yourself lost.

Stop. Take a deep breath, sit down if possible, calm yourself and recognize that whatever has happened to get you here is past and cannot be undone. You are now in a survival situation and that means . . .

Think. Your most important asset is your brain. Use it! Don't panic! Think first, so you have no regrets. Move with deliberate care. Take no action, even a footstep, until you have thought it through . . .

Observe. Take a look around you. Assess your situation and options. Take stock of your supplies, equipment, surroundings, and the capabilities of fellow survivors . . .

Plan. Prioritize your immediate needs and develop a plan to systematically deal with the emergency. Make a plan. Follow your plan. Adjust your plan only as necessary to deal with changing circumstances.[1] You will survive!

In a similar manner, we can take the S.T.O.P. acronym and use it as a spiritual guide for those who feel lost, broken, or confused.

S is for **Scripture.** When I'm most frightened, frustrated, heartbroken, or feeling lost in my spirit, the thing that helps me most is reading or reciting Scripture. The small, worn-out Bible I carry with me has been a source of strength and renews my faith. Hebrews 11 was given to Christians that we might be reminded of God's faithfulness in the past. That is why in my Bible I have several pages with dates, times, and places marked as to when God helped me through some ordeal. It reminds me of what He has done in the past so I can march forward with a promise for the future. The disciples had with them the Creator of Scripture, and He told them the truths that transformed their lives and helped them face many challenges with a sense of strength and security.

The apostle Peter couldn't have healed the crippled beggar (Acts 3) or preached his powerful sermon at Pentecost (Acts 2) without being empowered by the words and Spirit of Christ. What are you facing? Do you feel lost and confused? Think about getting into God's Word. A good place to look for how to handle your specific issue is the subject section or concordance in the back of a Bible. Use a word or subject that connects with your thought (e.g., trust, love, marriage, etc.) or need (peace, perseverance, patience, etc.)

T stands for **Truth**. Through the four Gospels, we read about our Master and Lord saying repeatedly to His disciples, "I tell you the truth . . . ." In His teachings, Jesus wanted to emphasize to His disciples truth from distorted thinking. The best way to determine if money is counterfeit is to study the real thing so that you can immediately spot false copies.

O is for **Obedience** to God's Word and the leading of the Holy Spirit. Being a committed disciple requires both faith *and* obedience. Like others, I often fail because I focus on the stresses of life rather than on God's faithfulness and provision (Matt. 14:22–31). Despite my human frailties, my faith in God's sovereignty is the cornerstone of my life and ministry. As believers, we are to be like Christ (Phil. 3:1–18).

P is for **Proclaiming** His Word and praising God for His grace and love. Matthew captured some motivating words from our Lord: "Whatever I tell you in the dark, speak in the light; and what you hear in the ear, preach on the housetops. And do not fear those who kill the body but cannot kill the soul. But rather fear Him who is able to destroy both soul and body in hell" (Matt. 10:27–28). If we believe Scripture, put our trust in Him who is able, and seek to be obedient, the natural by-product is to proclaim His Word to others. Why would we keep the good news to ourselves?

WHAT MAKES A GREAT FISHER OF MEN?

Unlike the disciples of old, we have many resources in most boats or within our packs to keep us on track. In a similar manner, God has filled our personal boats with all kinds of helpful tools to assist with the challenges of life. He has given us a whole range of helps so we can avoid being lost. In teaching His disciples, Jesus regularly reminded the guys about keeping focused on these four items: the Bible, the Holy Spirit, prayer, and fellowship.

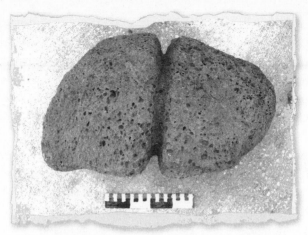

A grooved basalt boat anchor like used by ancient fishermen

THE BIBLE: A LAMP TO MY FEET

First, there is the Bible, which is like a map that guides and directs our lives. It helps us understand where we have been, where we are, and where we are going. It is an overview that enlightens us to the big picture and sets our course through uncharted waters, unexplored landscapes, and stormy seas. The Bible illuminates our path. The psalmist said, "Your word is a lamp to my feet and a light to my path" (Ps. 119:105). He also shared, "Your word I have hidden in my heart, that I might not sin against You" (Ps. 119:11). The Bible can and should be our map, our resource manual to chart the proper course for life. It does us very little good, however, *unless we follow it.*

THE HOLY SPIRIT: OUR INNER COMPASS

The Holy Spirit provides an inner compass to guide our conscience (Rom. 9:1). With the ever-changing moral codes of our society, it is helpful to know that the Holy Spirit is consistent from age to age. He will not fail us. When the Holy Spirit fills us, we are enabled to face the challenges and temptations before us . Jesus was "full of the Holy Spirit" and was "led by the Spirit." When Jesus was tempted in the desert the power of the same Spirit was with him (Luke 4:14). The word *power* is the same word used in Acts 1:8, where Jesus promised His disciples, "You will receive *power* when the Holy Spirit comes on you; and you will be my witnesses in Jerusalem, and in all Judea and Samaria, and to the ends of the earth." If we listen carefully to the quiet voice of the Holy Spirit, He will point us in the right direction (1 Cor. 2:12). We might say that we are like "flashlights," needing the "batteries" of the Holy Spirit to energize us for service and worship (Gal. 5:22–23). A flashlight without batteries cannot do what it is designed to do, and a Christian who is not yielded to the Holy Spirit cannot do what God intends. The Holy Spirit also functions as an internal guidance system. He is the best GPS available.

PRAYER: COMMUNICATING WITH GOD

Prayer is a special communication system with God Almighty. Through prayer, we can go to God and share our dreams, concerns, fears, ambitions, requests, and praise (Phil. 4:6). As a foghorn or a distant sound of a train in the woods helps direct a lost fisherman or woodsman to his destination, an active prayer life gives guidance and vision to help us through the fog of life. So important was prayer to Christ that He often withdrew from the crowds for the sole purpose of praying (Luke 5:16). Prayer was so important to His disciples' personal growth that Christ gave them a model prayer as a guide (Matt. 6:5–15).

In his booklet *How to Pray*, E. Stanley Jones tells us that "prayer is not only the refuge of the weak; it is the reinforcement of the strong."[2] Prayer isn't just for bluegill fishermen or lost boaters or hikers—*it's for you and me*. Remember, the greatest fisherman who ever lived—Jesus Christ—saturated His life with prayer (Mark 1:35; 6:46).

Jones goes on to suggest that "prayer is not bending God to my will, but it is a bringing of my will into conformity with God's will, so that His will may work in and through me."[3] You might look at it this way: When you are in a small boat and you throw out a boat hook to catch hold of the shore, do you pull the shore to yourself, or do you pull yourself to the shore? "Prayer is not bending the universe to your will, making God a cosmic bellhop for your purposes, but prayer is cooperating with the purposes of God to do things you never dreamed you could do."[4]

CHRISTIAN FELLOWSHIP: MUTUAL SUPPORT

Christian fellowship is another "navigational tool" the Lord has given to us for successful living. Throughout many years and many adventures, my fellowship with other believers has enabled me to face my fears with courage and support. Faithful and encouraging friends can strengthen us to face those uncharted waters. And fellow believers hold us accountable so we can grow and stay on course.

Fellowship is a major theme in 1 John 1. Such fellowship may take place both between a Christian and God and between a Christian and another Christian. "Fellowship" (*koinonia*) means to share in common, to participate, to experience unity. It is this unity that separates Christian fellowship from simple friendships. It is a bond that has eternal significance.

WHEN WE ARE LOST

Thinking back to the times when I've been lost, literally or figuratively, it was only by fixing my gaze upon the resources God provides that I was able to take a bad decision and find a positive outcome. So, too, using the navigational tools and resources Christ has given us helps us keep our lives on track. Keeping our personal priorities in order—with Christ Himself being the *top* priority—prevents us from sinking into the circumstances of daily living. *Christ will keep you from getting "lost in the fog."*

LET'S GO FISHING

Do you or someone you know feel lost? What adjustments do you need to make in your priorities or decision making? Do you access your map (Bible) to find direction? What is your "map" for living? List three scriptures that could serve as a guide in your life:

_____

_____

_____

Prayer is that communication with God that helps direct our ways. A good father will want to understand the desires and aspirations of his child. Our relationship with God works in a similar way, as our heavenly Father wants to enter into our deepest heartfelt yearnings. Being omnipotent and omnipresent, He already knows your deepest thoughts, but prayer allows us to admit our failures and praises to God so that He can shape our lives into His plan and will.

FISHING FOR MEN

Spend time with your mentoring partner reviewing the STOP acronym for disciples: Scripture, Truth, Obedience, and Proclaiming. Assess your own strengths and weaknesses, and those of your partner, in each of these areas. What needs to be strengthened? How can your strengths help your mentoring partner's weaknesses, and vice versa?

What are the resources you have in your spiritual toolbox? Can you think of any other resources that would help you share your testimony and faith? What resources does your mentor recommend?

If you were in a boat with Jesus, what questions would you have for Him? Can you discuss those questions with a friend who is knowledgeable of God's Word?

PERSEVERANCE IS DRIVEN BY PASSION

FISHING TALE

It is my opinion that throughout Christ's ministry, He endeavored to build three things into His disciples: be a disciple, make a disciple, and form churches that make disciples. The reality is that it takes leaders, men of spiritual courage and passion, to show the way for discipleship to occur. Think about it: all the disciples but John died a martyr's death. That speaks volumes to me about an attitude that embraces patience, perseverance, and passion. A good attitude is a necessity in all areas of life; a bad attitude is like a flat tire. When I think about hiring someone or developing deep personal friendships, I enjoy most the people who project an attitude of what I call the "three P's" (patience, perseverance, and passion). To be an effective spiritual mentor, you do not have to be a crazy "Type A" guy like me or the apostles Peter and Paul. With "charging" personalities comes a host of other baggage that isn't always welcomed by those whose hearts beat at a different pace. No matter what your personality type, I believe that God wants us to use our gifts, talents, knowledge, and personality in such a way that those who witness our lives can say, "There is a man of patience, perseverance, and passion."

One of my favorite fishing stories relates to a fishing adventure I had in the California Delta. An aspiring young pro asked me to accompany him on a half-day trip. He wanted to use his boat. The pro

61

Top: three Tiberius coins with marking of anchors. Bottom: larger coin is a silver stater like the one Peter used to pay the taxes for Jesus and himself (Matt. 17:24)

was seeking to utilize my background and experience on the delta as a guide to help him become a more effective fisherman for an upcoming bass tournament. After checking out a couple of my favorite spots with no success, we boated along for another mile scoping out other spots. In front of us was an old sunken barge probably forty-five feet long. This wooden relic had been submerged since World War II, when many of the abandoned ammunition barges were discarded in the delta. Over the course of many years, barnacles and crustaceans had built up on the boat, thereby attracting many small fish to the area. I believed this piece of structure had to have some good fish nearby, because there were no other good-looking spots within a mile. As we spent some time casting our plastic crawfish and worms along the length of this barge, I was shocked that we did not receive any bites. Not a bump nor hint of a fish.

As we got to the end of the barge, I decided to recast into an area where both of us had just worked. This time I waited a little longer before retrieving my lure. As I retrieved it, I shook my rod tip, thereby transmitting tremors onto the lure. Suddenly, I felt that notorious thud on the end of the line and reared back to hook a nice three-pound bass. My partner could not believe I caught the fish in the area we had just worked. I asked him to turn the boat around and we quickly motored back up to the beginning of the barge where we first started. With a puzzled look, my partner asked, "Why are we recasting in the same water we just fished?" I suggested that we hadn't properly fished the water because we had been short of perseverance, passion, and patience. I encouraged him to make every cast count.

As we continued fishing that wreck with a different attitude, we picked up another five fish. That happened because our attitude and methods changed. We were now convinced that fish were there and we worked the lures slower, now confident we would catch something.

A good fisherman knows that sometimes he must throw to the same spot several times before the fish will strike. Repeated presentations, using different lures and techniques, will often cause even the most stubborn and wary fish to finally become interested.

WHAT MAKES A GREAT FISHER OF MEN?

THE RIGHT ATTITUDE

Jesus didn't promise His disciples that sharing their faith would always be easy. He didn't hand them a bunch of tracts and tell them to go to the next village and hand them out. On the contrary, He reminded His followers that there would be times when they could be misunderstood, rebuked, challenged, abandoned, threatened, and in fear of their very lives. Most of us never have to face these types of abuses. The point is that these men were unwilling to compromise about what stirred their hearts.

A tournament fisherman develops a positive strategy and competitive desire to encourage both himself and his team on to victory. He must maintain a quiet confidence with every cast, believing that if the bait is worked correctly, he will successfully stimulate the fish to bite. Related to this, I think it is amazing to witness how excited fishermen can become when they find a new lure or product that creates excitement with the fish. They tell everyone they meet about "the good news" of their product discovery and how it is making an impact on the fishery.

A disciple needs the same positive, affirming, and even competitive attitude to be an encouragement to the unbeliever. We must be excited about the "product" we have to share—*the gospel that leads to eternal life.* Isn't it an embarrassment that the greatest news of all—eternal life through God's Son—should be kept a secret by so many of His disciples?

Ephesians 4:23 indicates that a proper attitude comes through a renewal of our minds, which suggests a complete change in our natural patterns of thinking. We naturally get excited about new fishing lures; perhaps part of the renewal process is to begin getting excited about the things that get God excited. In other words, renewing our minds means to learn to think as God thinks—and this renewal can only come from the Holy Spirit and by studying God's Word.

Scripture also tells us that we are to model the attitude of Christ in our daily lives (Phil. 2:5). Indeed, we are to focus our minds on "whatever things are true, whatever things are noble, whatever things are just, whatever things are pure, whatever things are lovely, whatever things are of good report, if there is any virtue and if there is anything praiseworthy—meditate on these things" (Phil. 4:8). For a disciple, it is *imperative* that we have an open and loving heart that manifests itself with an infectious attitude that attracts people to the Christ who is working in and through us.

So often, disciples make a single feeble attempt to share truth with a friend or neighbor and then become discouraged because their message was not initially received well. We quickly become disappointed with those who seem uninterested in God's Word. This is especially the case when we share our faith with relatives or close friends. It is admittedly difficult to discuss matters of spiritual significance with those closest to us. We often make the excuse that "we tried once and have fulfilled our discipleship duties." *But have we?* Did we persevere? *With patience?*

America's pastor and my friend Chuck Swindoll said this about attitude:

> The longer I live, the more I realize the impact of attitude on life. Attitude, to me, is more important than facts. It is more important than the past, than education, than money, than circumstances, than failures, than successes, than what other people think or say or do. It is more important than appearance, giftedness, or skill. It will make or break a company . . . a church . . . a home. The remarkable thing is we have a choice every day regarding the attitude we will embrace for that day. We cannot change the inevitable. The only thing we can do is play on the one string we have, and that is our attitude . . . I am convinced that life is 10% what happens to me, and 90% how I react to it. And so it is with you . . . we are in charge of our Attitudes."[1]

PERSEVERANCE

Long before the apostle Peter first cast his line into the Sea of Galilee, fishermen have been driven by the adventure and challenge of matching wits with our friends with fins. I recently saw a bumper sticker that summarizes an angler's fixation with fishing: "Fishing isn't a matter of life and death—it's more important than that."

Earlier in this book, I noted that fishermen have qualities that make them uniquely suited to be good spiritual mentors. Christ delighted in working with fishermen. They have a way of infecting others with their perseverance and passion while sharing techniques and skills that encourage others. The inner drive and zeal that accomplished fishermen bring to their sport is unparalleled in most other occupations. Like a good fisherman, a dedicated disciple is zealous and eager to share information that will help people catch the vision of the good news that brings everlasting life.

The story I provided about fishing the California Delta demonstrates a perseverance that allowed us to land several nice fish. It would have been easy to give up on the challenge, but perseverance paid off. Whether leading others, tackling life's problems, or contributing to some great cause, perseverance is crucial to success. The old saying "hang in there!" is more than an expression of encourage-ment—it is good advice for a disciple. On His second tour through Galilee, Jesus taught His disciples the parable of the sower as a way of encouraging them to persevere. He said, "But the ones that fell on the good ground are those who, having heard the word with a noble and good heart, keep it and bear fruit with *patience*" (Luke 8:15, emphasis added). Our "stick-to-it-iveness" has a lot to do with getting the right results—God's results. Many young Americans at the turn of the twentieth century learned this principle when they memorized this little verse from their McGuffey's Reader:

> The fisher who draws in his net too soon,
> Won't have any fish to sell;
> The child who shuts up his book too soon,
> Won't learn any lessons well.
> If you would have your learning stay,
> Be patient—don't learn too fast;
> The man who travels a mile each day,
> May get around the world at last.[2]

The witness of many of Christ's followers reminds us that we need to *persevere*. A good summation is found in Hebrews 12:1–2: "Therefore we also, since we are surrounded by so great a cloud of witnesses, let us lay aside every weight, and the sin which so easily ensnares us, and let us run with endurance the race that is set before us, looking unto Jesus, the author and finisher of our faith, who for the joy that was set before Him endured the cross, despising the shame, and has sat down at the right hand of the throne of God."

PASSION

Passion is the primary quality that drives perseverance. This is certainly what drove our perseverance to conquer the wits of the stubborn bass in the California Delta. Our passion for the sport transcended the challenges to hook a fish. For many of us, however, it's easier to talk about passion than to *find* it—or, having found it, to

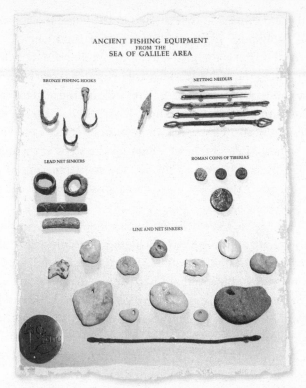

Author collection of some first century artifacts from the Sea of Galilee

maintain it. A spiritual mentor who takes his job seriously *must* have a passion for his work. Nothing challenges a person more than seeing a believer truly excited about his faith. Again, I must caution that it is not about having a robust cheerleader-type of personality. No, it is that inward drive and determination that sets a true mentor/disciple apart from someone who just shows up on Sunday morning for his hour fix of faith.

Gordon MacDonald wrote in his encouraging book *Restoring Your Spiritual Passion*, "Passion—the kind that causes some to excel beyond anyone else—dulls one's sense of fatigue, pain, and the need for pleasure or even well-being. Passion leads some to pay incredible prices to reach a goal of some sort. . . . A passion is necessary in the performance of Christian faith."[3]

This kind of passion is illustrated in the life of the apostle Paul. Indeed, Paul spoke from a wellspring of passion when he wrote, "Brethren, I do not count myself to have apprehended; but one thing I do, forgetting those things which are behind and reaching forward to those things which are ahead, I press toward the goal for the prize of the upward call of God in Christ Jesus" (Phil. 3:13–14). Many of us experience spiritual passion when we first receive Christ into our hearts by faith. Like the healed man on the steps at the temple in Jerusalem (Acts 3:8), we leap for joy, and sometimes our infectious zeal embarrasses those who have more (or less) experience in matters of faith.

As time sets in, some believers institutionalize and compartmentalize their faith and spend too much time identifying with folks who have lost the joy of their salvation. If we are not careful, we may end up like many one-dimensional Christians—*boring and uncaring*. Too often, believers can become inactive participants—mere spectators of life and of the lives around them. A mature Christian does not preclude passion, but learns to control or channel his emotions in a rational manner. He uses his passion as an engine to push his spiritual boat and to encourage others in their faith.

Most believers go through periods in which they find themselves lacking spiritual passion to one degree or another. We live in a hurried, stress-filled environment that tends to drain us of positive emotions. The busyness of our lifestyle absorbs what passion might exist. We find ourselves investing all our precious energies into events and programs of the public world. Meanwhile, our private world—the heart—starves for attention and encouragement. The more emphasis we place on *activities*, the less time we have for *devotion*. As MacDonald correctly observed, "Doing more *for* God may mean less time *with* God. Talking becomes an effective substitute for meditating or listening."[4]

Didn't Christ live a pressurized life? He only had about three and a half years to minister before He was taken away. But He never succumbed to the tyranny of the urgent. J. B. Phillips, in his book *Your God Is Too Small*, stated, "It is refreshing, and salutary, to study the poise and quietness of Christ. His task and responsibility might well have driven a man out of his mind. But He was . . . never a slave of the clock. He was acting, He said, as He observed God to act— never in a hurry."[5] Did Christ have passion? You bet He did, but it was balanced with humility and time for restoration.

Throughout the Gospels, we witness Christ withdrawing from the multitudes to be alone with the Father (Luke 5:16). He regularly recharged His spiritual batteries through prayer and meditation. While being driven by His passion and mission "to seek and to save that which was lost" (Luke 19:10), He was guided by a prudent spirit of control and internal balance.

Perhaps this is the model that John Wesley (1703–1791) used in balancing his work within reasonable limits. Wesley concluded, "Though I am always in haste, I am never in a hurry; because I never undertake any more work than I can go through with perfect calmness of spirit."[6] We would be wise to imitate Wesley's modus operandi.

PATIENCE

Whether a fisherman or spiritual mentor, we can persevere and have great passion, but at the end of the day if we don't have patience we will not be victorious. Some of us have relatives we love deeply who haven't come to faith; we fret, worry, become impatient, and sometimes even reach a point of frustration that comes out in a negative attitude. But look at what Christ modeled. Our Lord had many siblings and other relatives in Nazareth who didn't believe He was the Messiah. One time when He spoke in His hometown synagogue, the people (probably including some members of His family) tried to throw Him off a cliff (Luke 4:16–30). In an earlier instance, Jesus' family even said of Him, "He is out of His mind" (Mark 3:21).

But Jesus demonstrated a great deal of patience with those who scorned Him. Eventually, even His half brother James became a devout follower and penned these words: "My brethren, count it all joy when you fall into various trials, knowing that the testing of your faith produces patience. But let patience have its perfect work, that you may be perfect and complete, lacking nothing. . . . Blessed is the man who endures temptation; for when he has been approved, he will receive the crown of life which the Lord has promised to those who love Him" (James 1:2–4, 12). Throughout his epistle, James talks about "enduring," which is another word for "having patience."

Let's look at five ways we can become a more patient person.

1. Ask yourself what causes you to become impatient. Is it because you fear having things out of control? Are you willing to let go a bit and let God into your life and circumstances? Do you seek to have power over people or circumstances? What does that say about your faith in God and others? Can you delegate without feeling like things won't work out well? What are the triggers that set you off? What grace can you bring into the situation so you can allow others who may be less gifted than yourself to be free to be themselves?

2. Figure out how you process life and important decisions. It is important to know your experience, talents, gifts, personality, management style, and approach to problem solving. Your way is just that—it is *your* way. Someone else may process life and decisions differently. That does not make them wrong and you right. It just means that you are the way God made you, and they are the way God made them. We are different. Embrace our differences and learn from those who have dissimilar approaches.

3. When you become impatient with someone, think about what your expectations were and why you feel impatient. Go to God's Word and research verses that apply to the traits of your impatience. Pray that, through your modeling of hard work, the sluggard who frustrates you will be encouraged to work harder. Remember that our job isn't to fix people but to model Christ's love.

4. Prayer and meditation may sound simple, but they do work. And they *require* work—and they also require one of our most valuable resources: time. When you are frustrated and impatient with someone else or with yourself, take a break away from the

situation and practice some relaxation techniques and deep breathing while you pray upon the grace and patience God has given you. If you really concentrate and take the appropriate time, you will become a thankful person and put impatience on the back burner. This is, of course, an ongoing situation. The stress and strain of everyday life can create impatience over and over again. But as we practice prayer and meditation, we will slowly change our attitude and our tendency to be impatient with others and with situations.

5. Keep the big picture in mind. Often those of us who are perfectionists or look at details forget about the big picture. As Jesus told Martha in Luke 10:41–42, "Martha, Martha, you are worried and troubled about many things. But one thing is needed, and Mary has chosen that good part, which will not be taken away from her." Remember that our goal is to live a life pleasing to God, to become more like Christ every day, and to witness to and serve others—all of which require patience, perseverance, and passion.

LET'S GO FISHING

The disciples found the call of the Galilean carpenter to be irresistible. Once the fishermen met the Savior, the everyday task of setting nets became drudgery. They had always enjoyed their work and found it fulfilling, but now the fish began to stink, the mending of nets seemed trivial, and the hours of waiting in the boats became unbearable. They found their minds traveling back to fellowship around a campfire or Bible study at the feet of the Master. As they experienced more of Christ, their passion for challenging others with "the call" became all-consuming. They had a vision for reaching the world, not just Judea and Samaria.

To be sure, there were times when the disciples—like each of us—became discouraged and waned in their passion and vision. One such occasion was immediately after the crucifixion. In John

21, we find Simon Peter and the other disciples at a point of physical and mental exhaustion. They witnessed their leader killed and were forced to endure all the stress-filled events surrounding His death. Judas's betrayal of the Lord (Matt. 26:47–56), Peter's threefold denial of Christ (26:69–75), and the subsequent trial (27:11–32) had left the disciples without hope or passion. And because they were without passion, their perseverance waned, and their patience dissipated.

In their discouragement, they did the only thing they knew how to do—*they went fishing.* But even as they were fishing, the risen Jesus gloriously appeared and caught their attention on the Sea of Galilee (John 21:1–11). He encouraged them and reshaped their thinking by helping them refocus their vision for ministry and their calling. *They were to be fishers of men.* Jesus instructed them, "Therefore go and make disciples of all nations, baptizing them in the name of the Father and of the Son and of the Holy Spirit, and teaching them to obey everything I have commanded you" (Matt. 28:19–20 NIV).

Christ restored and reenergized the disciples' spiritual passion. And as their passion was fanned back into a flame, so their will to persevere was renewed within them. They were now ready to face any challenge, knowing that the risen Christ would be with them always. Of course, merely knowing about the need to have passion and a vision is not enough. One must be willing to *apply* the lessons learned and *actively participate* in the discipling process.

FISHING FOR MEN

That is what the discipling process is all about—getting involved, being passionate about our calling, and being persistent in applying all we know. Spend time together with your mentoring partner studying the process of Jesus' mentoring with the disciples in the gospel of John. Consider the following verses: John 8:31; 13:35; 15:8. Discuss three things that you could do, together or individually, to enhance your spiritual passion.

OVERCOMING DOUBT AND OBSTACLES

FISHING TALE

In our two-engine chartered plane, we were rapidly descending through thick clouds at two hundred miles per hour. The majestic mountain peaks of the Alaskan Range, including the great Mount McKinley at 20,320 feet, pushed through the cloud cover like shark's teeth in a sea of foam. Our approach was dropping us into a canyon that contained the chilly waters of Lake Iliamna. If everything worked the way it was planned, we would come out of the clouds five hundred feet above the middle of the lake.

The wings of the plane began to chatter in the icy air as the plane continued to descend. The plane fluttered in the turbulence as my fishing buddies strained to see anything through the white mist surrounding us. Casual conversation stopped and rapid breathing took its place. In a matter of seconds, the emotion of fear became our in-flight companion.

Fear penetrates the heart with questions of doubt and mistrust of the unknown and the unseen. Even the combat-hardened Vietnam War vet traveling with us began to feel the essence of fear that consumed the cockpit, as perspiration began to flow freely. Fear can grip people like a man-eating shark embedding its teeth into soft flesh. It can rip and tear away chunks of faith and inner peace from the body of life. When such fear strikes, saints begin to confess their sins, and even some atheists suddenly seek the comfort of the Creator.

Doubt is a partner of fear. They feed off one another like blood-sucking parasites. Have you ever wrestled with them? They creep into our lives without regard to position, power, or authority. There are all kinds of doubt and fear—we can doubt that a friend will be faithful, doubt that the bus will arrive on time, doubt that we will catch a fish. One reason for doubt is that we have been disappointed in the past. Fear, on the other hand, can be a more captivating thought, as we might actually have instinctive fears—of heights, flying, rejection, crowds, the dark, being alone, financial failure, dying, and much more. Maybe you have experienced one of these foes.

Fear can grip us in ways that often seem merciless. If we allow it to consume us, fear can rob us of our effectiveness. Our spiritual might can be turned into quivering flesh once fear and doubt close their tight jaws on our lives. Clearly there were numerous occasions when the original disciples had moments of doubt and fear. Imagine having seen your leader (Christ) being tortured and then hung on a cross. Not only are the Roman soldiers your enemy, but now a host of your Jewish neighbors and friends, who could not grasp the promises of Christ, are tracking down Jesus' followers and killing them. I think that might create some anxious moments for anyone aligned with Christ and His followers.

I selected this topic to place in a manual on discipleship because so many men I meet are inwardly battling with some components of doubt and fear. The prophetic times we live in and the recent struggles about so many critical things (health care, terrorists, financial collapses, school violence, divorce, etc.) has stolen a great deal of joy from those who struggle with this two-headed demon. Disciples of Christ need to honestly confront those issues in our lives.

Being a Christian doesn't exempt us from trouble and challenges. In fact, I submit that being a conservative evangelical today requires a great deal of courage. It is for that reason Christ tried to prepare His original twelve disciples through the Sermon on the

Mount. Many times Jesus told His followers not to have fear as they faced inevitable challenges (Matthew 10:26, 28, 31; Luke 12:7, 32).

WHAT MAKES A GREAT FISHER OF MEN?

The transparency of the Gospels testifies to us that disciples are not exempt from the doubting moments and the pain of fear. And while I've briefly discussed the two occasions when Christ utilized His power to calm the sea, let's dig a little deeper into these important events. On two separate occasions, Jesus used the stormy waters of the Sea of Galilee to remind His disciples of the lessons taught in Psalm 27. This psalm contains a potent repellent to the "shark attacks" of fear—"Whom shall I fear? The LORD is the strength of my life; of whom shall I be afraid?" (v. 1). In Mark 6:45–51, we find the disciples returning before nightfall from the miraculous feeding of five thousand people, and Jesus bids them to go back to Bethsaida, on the other side of the lake.

On another occasion, we find Jesus, along with Peter and his fishing friends, crossing the lake (Matt. 8:24–27). Again, a winter evening storm emerged and assaulted the disciples—this time while boating from Capernaum to Kursi located on the eastern shore. The storm that came up on the Sea of Galilee that day would have been the equivalent of a tsunami; it was like an earthquake on water, what we today would term a "perfect storm."

Today's Galilean fishermen tell us that such storms on the Kinnereth (Galilee area) are common during the winter. These well-known eastern storms, called *Sharkia* in Arabic (meaning *shark*), have always caused apprehension among fishermen. Christ used these "stormy water adventures" to establish and increase the disciples' faith in His deity. When the disciples asked the rhetorical question, "What kind of man is this?" (Matt 8:27 NIV), they were acknowledging Christ's deity and power. Although miracles are hard for modern man to accept, the New Testament is clear that

Jesus is Lord not only over His church but also over all creation. The disciples recognized that Christ could control the realm of nature, proving that He was God.

FEAR DEVELOPS FAITH AND CHARACTER

It is very important, during times of fear and anxiety, to remind ourselves of one vital truth: the vast majority of things we fear never come to pass! Remember my opening story about my impending airplane crash? In that situation, it was only natural that everyone inside that little airplane should become frightened—after all, it appeared that the plane was going to crash.

But it didn't. Here's what actually happened on that icy day: The pilot plotted the boundaries of the lake on his GPS, then did a downward spin until he broke through the low clouds at about 150 feet above the icy water. The airplane was still hampered by ice, but despite the rattling and chattering of the wings the pilot was able to wrestle it back under control. We leveled off, regained our bearings—and the entire group of passengers let out a cheer. Our prayers were answered and the stress felt by all was relieved until our next adventure.

Fear can help develop both faith and character in the life of a Christian. Let me illustrate this with a fish story. As easterners transplanted themselves to the West Coast, they found themselves longing for the East Coast cod. It was often shipped by rail to several fine dining restaurants on the West Coast. The customers, though, complained that the fish just weren't the same. Despite providing aerated containers with water from the original source, the fish arrived soft and tasteless. Then someone reckoned that the fish needed to be challenged in a real-life environment. Catfish or bullheads were among the natural predators of the cods and were introduced into the shipping containers. From that time forward, the fish arrived firm and tasty. *Life without some stress presents no challenges to mature our faith and firm up our convictions.* Real living involves dealing with the catfish of life. It is healthy for us to encounter people and circumstances that challenge us and refine our character. Through these challenges, we are able to test our faith and witness God's miracles. The raging waters of our lives will be calmed as we rest in God's sovereign hands. If we focus on the Lord and His promises, we will not be robbed of joy in our lives, despite the circumstances.

Popular author and pastor Chuck Swindoll tells us that worry, stress, and fear can be joy stealers.

> Worry is an inordinate anxiety about something that may or may not occur. It has been my observation that what is being worried about usually does not occur. But worry eats away at joy like slow-working acid while we are waiting for the outcome. . . .
>
> Stress is a little more acute than worry. Stress is intense strain over a situation we cannot change or control—something out of our control. . . . And instead of releasing it to God, we churn over it. It is in that restless churning stage that our stress is intensified. Usually the thing that plagues us is not as severe as we make it out to be.
>
> Fear, on the other hand, is different from worry and stress. It is dreadful uneasiness over the presence of danger, evil, or pain. As with the other two, however, fear usually makes things appear worse than they really are.[1]

The concept of being fearful isn't anything to be ashamed of. Know that when those times come, even to the most mature believer, we have the comfort of the Holy Spirit and God's Word to help us pass through the darkness of the event.

LET'S GO FISHING

As spiritual mentors who may have been through some trials, tribulations, and major testing, we can share with those we disciple the importance of staying grounded in God's Word, prayer, and meditation. We need to keep things in perspective. If we focus on our fears, they always appear bigger and worse than they really are. But if we focus on God's sovereign control, fear is kept in check and God uses our experiences to mature our faith. Faith can dispel fear, but only in proportion to its strength. As the faith of the disciples grew, their strength to overcome their fears also increased.

We need to relax in the promises Christ gave His first-century disciples. During His farewell discourse prior to His betrayal, Jesus comforted His disciples by saying, "Let not your heart be troubled; you believe in God, believe also in Me" (John 14:1). Moreover, Jesus said, "Peace I leave with you, My peace I give to you; not as the world gives do I give to you. Let not your heart be troubled, neither let it be afraid" (v. 27).

The disciples' belief in these wonderful promises allowed them to mature in their faith. They were able to declare their assurance in Christ and victory over fear in their ministries. The following are some verses that are especially helpful when I've been confronted with fearful situations:

> For God has not given us a spirit of fear, but of power and of love and of a sound mind. (2 Tim. 1:7)

> So we may boldly say:
>
>> "The LORD is my helper;
>> I will not fear.
>> What can man do to me?" (Heb. 13:6)

> For you did not receive the spirit of bondage again to fear, but you received the Spirit of adoption by whom we cry out, "Abba, Father." (Rom. 8:15)

> There is no fear in love; but perfect love casts out fear, because fear involves torment. But he who fears has not been made perfect in love. (1 John 4:18)

GOD'S RECIPE FOR DEALING WITH "SHARK ATTACKS"

One of the best recipes for attacking fear can be found in Psalm 27. David's numerous struggles with fearful situations qualify him to be a "wise counselor" to all of us. Consider his words about how to reduce fear: "The LORD is my light and my salvation—whom shall

I fear? The LORD is the stronghold of my life—of whom shall I be afraid?" (v. 1 NIV). This psalm is virtually brimming with spiritual gems. To summarize David's eloquent expressions, we can sift the following truths that can be used to fight off attacks of fear:

* **Seek God's Protection:** "For in the time of trouble He shall hide me in His pavilion; in the secret place of His tabernacle He shall hide me; He shall set me high upon a rock" (v. 5).

* **Worship God's Majesty:** "I will sing, yes, I will sing praises to the LORD" (v. 6).

* **Pray:** "Hear, O LORD, when I cry with my voice! Have mercy also upon me, and answer me" (v. 7).

* **Focus on the Lord:** "Your face, LORD, I will seek" (v. 8).

* **Study God's Word:** "Teach me Your way, O LORD, and lead me in a smooth path, because of my enemies" (v. 11).

* **Be Confident:** "I would have lost heart, unless I had believed that I would see the goodness of the LORD in the land of the living" (v. 13).

* **Be Patient:** "Wait on the LORD" (v. 14).

* **Be Courageous:** "Be of good courage, and He shall strengthen your heart; wait, I say, on the LORD" (v. 14).

FISHING FOR MEN

Spend time with your mentoring partner making a list of the things you are fearful or anxious about at present. Then make another list of the things you are thankful for. Finally, spend time together putting Philippians 4:6 into practice.

If we are to be effective as mentors and strong leaders of our families, we must learn to cope with fear and tribulation. What are three fears that try to rob you of a joyful life?

Why should we fear not? Is God bigger than our fears?

Three styles of bronze fishing hooks from the time of Christ

How do God's comforting words help you overcome your fears (Pss. 27:2; 91:1; Isa. 51:12–16; Rom. 8:15; 2 Tim. 1:7; 1 John 4:18)?

Fear can cause us to doubt and doubt can cause us to be fearful. What are some practical things you could do to overcome your fears? Here are a few suggestions:

✳ Write down your fear(s)—in detail—on a piece of paper.

✳ Write down the worst-case scenario you can imagine.

✳ Ask yourself, "What is the real possibility of this happening?"

✳ Then ask yourself this question—"Why am I scaring myself in my head?"

✳ Change the tape in your head—begin to erase it. Replace it with Philippians 4:6–7: "Be anxious [fearful] for *nothing*, but in *everything* by *prayer* and *supplication*, with *thanksgiving*, let your requests be made known to God; and the peace of God, which surpasses all understanding, will guard your hearts and minds through Christ Jesus" (emphasis added).

✳ Continue to change out the tape by repeating Philippians 4:6–7 over and over.

✳ Look at your written material and decide what *good* could come from the situation as you overcome your fear.

Quote Romans 8:28 to yourself—and believe it. "And we know that all things work together for good to those who love God, to those who are the called according to His purpose."

WE CAN'T FILL THE NETS ALONE

FISHING TALE

Whether or not you are a fisherman, the following stories have major implications on being a successful disciple and why working with a body of believers is so important. You can replace the fishing metaphors with your own, but don't lose the significance of being a team player.

When you consider the challenge that fishermen had back in the first century, it was no picnic to go fishing. Just handling all the gear, rigging, and nets was exhausting. It is interesting to note that the same netting methods used by the ancient fisherman can still be seen in practice on the Sea of Galilee. If you were to embark on a fishing trip with the first-century disciples, you would not find them using graphite rods with high-retrieve level-wind reels. The equipment our fishing forefathers used was crude but very effective.

Today, people can visit the House of Anchors at the Kibbutz Ein Gev, located on the eastern shoreline of the Sea of Galilee. There are wonderful artifacts dating back to the time of Christ that clearly depict the type of fishing equipment that was available to the disciples. In addition to the ancient hooks, sinkers (stone and lead), line, and nets, you will see a large display of boat anchors that help the modern-day angler connect with his spiritual and fishing roots.

קטע של רשת מימי 'בר-כוכבא'.
נמצא ב'מערת-האגרות' במדבר-יהודה.

Portion of net from 'Bar-Kohba' period,
found in a cave near the Dead Sea.

Ancient Net from the 2nd century similar to those used by the disciple fishermen

Very little fishing was done in biblical times with a hook and line because this method was not particularly effective or efficient. Today, as you roam the shores of the Sea of Galilee, you will still find the majority of fishermen using the same netting strategies used two thousand years ago.

The hook-and-line angler is a very unfamiliar scene, representing perhaps only 1–2 percent of the fishermen on the lake. Angling as we know it is only mentioned once in the Gospels, and then not in connection with ordinary fishing (Matt. 17:24–27). In this passage, we find Peter being prodded by Jesus to go down to the shoreline and cast in his line. Peter's faith and God's miracle provided a specific fish with a silver coin in its mouth, which was used to pay the temple tax for both Jesus and himself.

I am indebted to archeologist Mendel Nun, the patriarch fisherman of Israel, for his thoughts regarding the netting strategies described below. He is recognized as a leading authority on ancient fishing techniques. The following techniques all relate in some way to specific teachings of Christ.

THE TRAMMEL NET (GILL NET)

The trammel net is the only one used in ancient times that is still predominant on the lake today. By intertwining three layers of netting, varying in mesh size, a long net is constructed that varies in height and length. It is constructed with a buoyant top line and weighted bottom line, thereby creating a wall that fish run into. This type of net requires a tremendous amount of mending and repair to keep it in proper shape. In the trammel net, the very mesh becomes wrapped around the gills of the fish, causing them to suffocate and die within the net's grasp. The net is then retrieved, and the fish are pulled from it and sorted accordingly. A good night's catch could bring up to two hundred pounds of fish, if the net was properly located in a strategic area.[1] The disciples used this type of net in Luke 5:1–7.

Once again, I appreciate Christ's practical approach of communicating with His disciples. He related His teachings to things that would be easily understood by those He was trying to reach. Though He was the most scholarly rabbi of His time, He did not try to become too theological or philosophical with these simple fishermen. Christ is always seen thinking of others.

THE CAST NET

Matthew 4:18 describes a person casting a net into the sea. The net referred to here, a "cast net," is shaped like a large circle (six to eight yards in diameter) and could be used from the shore or a boat. This net would be thrown or "cast" into a spot where fish were thought to be congregating. As the net opened to its full circumference, the lead or rock weights on the perimeter of the circular net caused it to collapse around the unsuspecting fish. The bottom line was then drawn tight, entrapping the fish. Our Lord used this analogy to encourage His disciples to gather men for salvation and to become "fishers of men."[2]

THE SEINE (DRAGNET)

From the shores of Tabgha, a suburb of Capernaum, located on the northern shoreline, we find Christ describing to His disciples an allegory of the kingdom of heaven: "Again, the kingdom of heaven is like a dragnet that was cast into the sea and gathered some of every kind, which, when it was full, they drew to shore; and they sat down and gathered the good into vessels, but threw the bad away" (Matt. 13:47–48).

This fits exactly the function of the seine or dragnet. The dragnet is made of netting shaped like a long wall, typically 250 to 300 yards long and three to four yards high. Most often, these nets were set early in the morning or late in the evening when the fish would frequent the shallow water areas.[3] This netting technique could not be worked by a single person, but required a group of fishermen.

After attaching one end to the shoreline, the boat would then make a large circle in the sea. Cork floats held the top of the net up in the water as the rock or lead weights pulled the bottom line of the net to the floor of the lake. After all of the net was fed out the back of the boat, the fishermen would bring the remaining end back to shore, where another group of fishermen would take the line. As the two groups of shore fishermen pulled the net onto the bank, the enclosed area became smaller with each passing moment.

The net moved through the water like a vertical wall bringing in a conglomerate of creatures. It was unforgiving, encompassing virtually everything in its sphere of reach. After the net was dragged up on the shore, the handlers sorted everything out. This was a consuming and detailed task that required a great deal of accuracy. The good fish were put into vessels or baskets, sometimes with water to keep them fresh and alive for the marketplace. The "bad" fish—probably carp (because they were bony) and catfish (the Levitical law prohibited eating fish without scales [Lev. 11:9])—were destroyed, not to be caught again.

WHAT MAKES A GREAT FISHER OF MEN?

As modern-day disciples, it is important that we use practical illustrations to share with people the basic truths that transform lives.

There are several styles and approaches to spiritual mentoring and discipleship, just as there are assorted nets to catch fish. Many books have been written that address the various techniques and strategies involved. At the risk of oversimplifying the subject, I would like to suggest that there are at least three styles of spiritual mentoring that are being used by Christians today. To some degree, we can see these styles represented in the kinds of nets our ancient fishermen friends used.

THE ENTRAPMENT METHOD: TRAMMEL NET

You invite an unsaved friend to a Christian event without telling him there will be some intense preaching as part of the program. You have driven him and his family to the event and have lost your keys in the parking lot. There is no cell phone coverage in the sanctuary and the doors have been locked. The two six-foot-eight greeters at the back of the room look like unhappy defensive linemen. There is no way for your visitors to escape—*they are trapped.*

In an effort to be cordial, the pastor asks your guests to stand up and introduce themselves to the crowd. Just after your friends have mopped up the puddle of perspiration from around their chairs, the usher sticks an offering plate in their face and suggests that a gift would be in order.

Do we wonder why these neighbors never speak to you again and have staked out a pit bull on their front yard? A little absurd? Perhaps! But often, in our passion to "save souls" or disciple a person, we do not think through how our customs may offend, frighten, or even disengage a person searching for truth. Evangelical pastors from "seeker sensitive" churches tell us that the two most threatening things a newcomer can be asked to do is address a group of strangers and give away their money. Let's face it: the potential for intimidation is great in certain churches.

Large church events certainly have their place, but they often fail to yield positive results with unsuspecting friends who do not know Jesus. To many of these people, the entrapment process feels like the trammel net described earlier. The unsuspecting visitor swims into a net of excitement and programs that end up strangling him into submission. Most often, any decisions made in this setting are short-lived and insincere.

Encourage your church to plan outreach events that present a comfortable, relaxed atmosphere. This is especially true with men. It is always good to use the outdoor environment or a community facility whenever possible. These are the least threatening and most comfortable places for the unbeliever. You can then gradually introduce them to your church facilities.

At first, avoid structured presentations and make sure there are plenty of happy, joyful Christians who can be introduced to your friends. Make it a point to know your guest's occupation, hobbies, and interests. Find someone in your church who shares those experiences, and make sure they have some informal time to talk with one another.

You should take responsibility for introducing your visitors to others. And be sure to mention to your visitors that *they are your guests* and should not worry about putting anything in the offering basket—*that is for church members only.* If your visitors feel you have been protective of their interests, they will be more receptive to an invitation to attend another program.

THE SMOTHERING METHOD: CAST NET

In our zeal to see a lost one saved or discipled, we develop an encompassing strategy that surrounds the unbeliever with considerable information and confrontations. We are sure to buy him a copy of the latest "Jesus book," while weekly encouraging him to attend church with us.

Our unbelieving friends often feel trapped and engulfed. They try to be kind and keep us as friends, but they can't stand our religiosity. Moreover, our inconsistent walk gets in the way of a reasonable evaluation of God's Word. Much like the cast net described earlier in the chapter, unbelievers are always looking for the net to be flung and the smothering to occur. Their best defense is to keep a healthy distance from anyone who might be a suspected "fisherman."

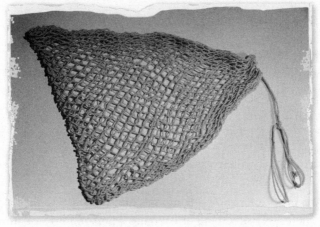

Casting net similar to what they used in the first century

People can sense insincerity. If you have a relationship with them simply to "save a soul," your phoniness will eventually surface and you will be discovered. People must first learn to love and respect us; *then* we have earned the right to share the love of Jesus with them.

Remember what we learned earlier about being a spiritual mentor. It is a journey that starts with an intentional relationship, a "come and see" attitude. As people feel your passion and compassion, the Holy Spirit will open doors of opportunity to share His Word.

As I write this chapter, I'm thinking about an unsaved friend whom I've gone hunting with, and I have asked him to come over and watch a football game. I like being with this guy. We share many similar interests and hobbies. Once when he was sick, I brought him a couple of meals. No sermon, no tract attached, no expectations, and no hidden agenda. My wife and I were just trying to love him so that he might see a little bit of Jesus in our hospitality.

It is not up to me to bring him to Jesus. That is up to the Holy Spirit. My responsibility is to love people and pray for them. As God opens doors of opportunity, I need to share my testimony (story) and find ways to connect with his spirit. It is the job of the spiritual mentor to try and identify the spiritual hole in a man's heart that could be filled with a relationship with the living God.

THE SANE METHOD: SEINE (DRAGNET)

The seine (dragnet) approach to capturing fish is by far the most forgiving and humane. The net is *slowly* moved around the fish to avoid scaring them. As the net is drawn closer to the fish, they have the freedom to go around or jump over the net and escape. The caring fisherman usually leaves enough net in the water that a pool of live fish is left for sorting. Should the net reach the shoreline with the captured fish, there exists a chance for the fish to be returned to the sea.

This provides a good analogy for our approach to discipleship. Other methods risk forcing or coercing a person into a relationship with Christ, but Jesus does not force anyone to accept Him as Lord and Savior. Just as a seine net allows fish an escape route, so also a more "sane" approach to discipleship permits an uninterested person to decline our invitation.

We must be models of the truth. It is our genuine love and concern that will first attract people's attention. We encourage their further exploration and consideration by being available and providing encouragement as opportunities present themselves. We must remember that people will accept Jesus into their hearts when they see the value of a personal relationship with the living God, but they are less likely to do so if they feel pressured or coerced. When they realize the emptiness in their lives and the lack of a cementing agent to hold their family together, *then* they are ready to be counseled and instructed on the biblical truths that transform.

Of course, it is not up to us to pass judgment on any individual. We are simply tools in the hands of the Master, being used to help shape and encourage others in their spiritual growth. Again, the prodding of the Holy Spirit is the primary motivating agent in the process.

Another important factor is that *teamwork* is the best way to handle a net or to influence an unbeliever or young Christian. Don't become prideful that your way is the best way or that only you can do it. Romans 12 and 1 Corinthians 12 remind us that, in the kingdom, we all have gifts and that we need to work together if we are going to be effective. Sometimes it might mean that you are mentoring an individual who has needs that you can't identify with, and you help him connect with another mentoring partner whose gifts are better suited. It might mean that you bring a group of people and resources around a guy or family.

I remember a time, early in my ministry, when I met with a couple who was having major problems. The guy was into drinking and staying out late, was a terrible money manager, and had a few other issues going against him. The wife nagged at him and regularly turned the kids against him. After meeting with them a couple of times, I could see that I was in over my head. I went to some mature Christians in my church and got a team to work with the couple. They came to me for general pastoral counseling on spiritual matters. An accountant friend of mine helped them develop a workable budget and encouraged the couple with resources developed by one of the nation's top Christian financial advisors. We had a female Christian psychologist meet with the wife on a regular basis. The youth pastor was brought in to help the kids through the mess.

We approached the matter as a team. Getting several people involved in more complex cases is an important thing in developing accountability that leads to successful living.

LET'S GO FISHING

For most people, coming into fellowship with Jesus is a *process*. It involves a series of God-ordained appointments and happenings for people to mature in their hearts so that, when the invitation is given, they willingly accept it. Yes, we have all heard of people who've had a "come to Jesus moment," like the former Hell's Angel dope addict who was riding down the highway at eighty miles an hour, fell off his bike, hit the pavement, and heard Jesus speak to him about his life. These type of "foxhole conversions" are real and for many have tremendous application when witnessing to the unsaved.

But don't feel that, unless your testimony is a spectacular tongue-speaking moment, you are just plain, ordinary Bob. Most of the people sharing their testimonies during a baptismal ceremony testify that their lives have been changing over the course of time and suddenly they come to accept the truth set before them. They most often accept Jesus as their Savior because they saw Him in *someone like you*—a spiritual mentor.

How did you come to accept Jesus? What were the motivating factors that brought you closer to God? How could you share those experiences and stories with others?

HOW TO ESTABLISH AND MAINTAIN A GOOD RELATIONSHIP WITH THE NEW CHRISTIAN AND THE NON-CHRISTIAN

If you are serious about making discipleship a part of your personal ministry and becoming a fisher of men (spiritual mentor), it is important to adhere to some basic practices that can help you attain dramatic results. The disciple-fishermen of the first century were successful with their nets because they knew how to use them effectively. The nets worked because of the meticulous preparation provided ahead of time. Careful attention was given to mending, restoring, and setting the nets. So it must be with discipleship—*we must prepare ourselves ahead of time*. Constant prayer and forethought are required to be successful at fishing for souls. The following suggestions may be helpful as you disciple.

1. Be faithful in praying regularly for the person you are discipling (Phil. 4:6).

2. Show genuine personal interest. The individual needs to feel that he is important to you and know that you are available to assist him with his journey. Be sure to ask, "How are things going for you?" People learn best when a personal need is met. As you show interest, ask questions and listen. You will become aware of this person's real concerns. Then you can sensitively share how Jesus is relevant to every detail of every human life. Remember, *concern for the person is more important than getting through the resources you are providing.* Be flexible in the Spirit!

3. Extend your interest beyond the follow-up meetings. Begin to build a friendship by doing things together—things you both enjoy, like fishing, hunting, photography, going to a game, playing video games, or just hanging out. Offer an invitation to do something fun with other Christians.

4. Share your own life as well as the message (Rev. 12:11).

- Be an example of worthy conduct (Phil. 4:9).
- Be open about how you are learning to apply the Bible in your life. Describe what God is teaching you. Be transparent (Rom. 12:3).
- When you're together, be natural in talking to God about your concerns (Rom. 12:9–10).
- Respond with excitement at any new spiritual enlightenment made by the individual you are mentoring. Be careful not to deflate his interest by treating God's Word as old or familiar. Be excited as you explore His Word together (Col. 3:16).[1]

5. Make special note of the following tips:

- Accept the individual on the basis of love and trust, not performance.

- Smile a lot, maintain eye contact, and use the person's name.
- Never laugh at a question or an answer.
- Never be negative about any other person, group, or organization.
- Approach follow-up on the basis of *sharing* rather than *teaching* (Phil. 2:3–4). Admit when you do not know an answer. Look it up together or find the answer later.
- *Be enthusiastic.* Your attitude is contagious (2 Cor. 9:2).

6. If the individual does not have a modern paraphrase of the Bible, offer to lend one of yours, or go together to a bookstore to buy one. The Voice or Living Bible are good choices for a non-Christian.

FISHING FOR MEN

When I first went into ministry, I adopted a discipling approach that a couple of my mentors used. It wasn't that the style was bad, but it wasn't who I was or what I did best. It is important to use an approach to people and mentoring that fits who you are. What form of outreach do you wish to adopt as your mentoring style and why?

Work together with your mentoring partner to analyze your spiritual journey and try to identify past milestones and set some new ones. If you don't continue to strive to be Christlike, you will be like a seed in the ground that never blossoms. Identify three milestones that you could set as a goal during the next twelve months (e.g., "I will follow a plan to read the entire Bible," "I will intentionally seek out opportunities to connect with someone not as spiritually mature and help them discover a deep walk with Jesus," or "I will find a spiritual mentor who can help me grow.")

What does it mean to be a new creature? Read 2 Corinthians 5:17. How do you apply this in your life?

As you go before God in prayer, ask Him to show you your weaknesses and how you could be a better example of the examined life under the conviction of the Holy Spirit.

THE **OBEDIENT**
DISCIPLE

FISHING TALE

With love and respect, I recount a wonderful fishing story that my friend the late Adrian Rogers told me. He was the pastor of one of the largest churches in America, Bellevue Baptist Church in Memphis, Tennessee. Through his television program *Love Worth Finding* and the Adrian Rogers Pastor Training Institute, he has reached millions.

It was the 1930s and times were tough for the Rogers household. The Great Depression bore down on folks like the Black Plague. Interestingly, fishing was one sport that experienced a resurgence during this difficult period in history. People took to their local fishing holes more for survival than merely entertainment or recreation. Such was the case for the hardworking patriarch of the Rogers family.

Being raised in West Palm Beach had its privileges for Adrian and his brother, including helping dad catch bluefish off the surf. Both children would catch small baitfish using pieces of crab or clams. The boys' dad would rig the small fish on a separate rod, then cast into the surf. The three would join in on landing the feisty fish.

A hastily made campfire and black skillet were all the trio needed to enjoy a good ol' fish fry, with a can of pork and beans as accompaniment. The warm evening sunsets provided a backdrop for the family to discuss God's beautiful creation and plan for mankind.

THE CALL OF GOD

As a young man, Adrian felt called to the ministry. His giftedness as an excellent Bible teacher and his obedient heart directed him to serve in several Florida Baptist churches. Each time he was recruited by a church, Adrian carefully measured the call against the direction of the Holy Spirit. His goal was not to become the leader of the largest denomination in the United States, but to understand and obey his Master's leading.

When the First Baptist Church of Merritt Island called Adrian, he recognized a unique opportunity to pastor some top scientists and astronauts associated with projects at Kennedy Space Center. But, most importantly, he felt God's hand in the placement and accepted the challenge to shepherd this unique congregation.

Adrian recalled those days as very challenging, with very little time off. "I've never worked so hard. These folks really placed a load on the senior pastor and I tried to respond accordingly." After about a year and a half, one of his men insisted that he take a break and go fishing. They packed up their gear and drove to a restricted area near the primary launch pad at the Cape. Clearance was given for these guys to enter a small beach area, where they could wade and fish in the shallow water. Within minutes, each man went his own way and Adrian started casting a MirrOlure with his old Mitchell spinning combo. With the big Florida blue sky above and numerous water birds filling the air, Adrian soaked up the peace and quiet.

Several hours passed without a single strike. Where were the fish? Each step and cast brought new anticipation but without success. Adrian looked up and said, "Lord, I have tried to be obedient and have sought to faithfully serve You. It would really do my heart good, that out of Your kindness I could catch a fish—any ol' fish will do." As Adrian lowered his head, he spotted a dark pocket just ahead of him. He moved a few steps toward the sink hole and placed his lure right in the center. Unsure of the depth, he allowed the lure to settle for several seconds, then began to slowly reel. Just as the lure was about to clear the dark hole, he spotted another shadow—and

Larger anchors (mooring stones) like these were used to tie boats off shore

this one was moving at a fast rate of speed. The large yellow mouth of a speckled trout opened and engulfed the MirrOlure.

The spunky sea-trout took off, peeling several yards of frayed line from the dusty reel. After several runs and some shouts of joy, Adrian wrestled the trophy-sized trout ashore. "The thrill and adrenaline rush that comes from such a battle is one of the things that inspires all anglers," Adrian recounted. "It was one of those awesome experiences that you never forget. I really felt it was more than a coincidence that this fish hit right after I prayed, so I thought I would try it again. I said, 'Lord, that was wonderful. I really enjoyed the experience and wonder if You could provide another one of those monster fish for me. If You can guide that miracle fish to the apostle Peter's hook, then I believe You can do the same for me."

Adrian made a second cast into the same spot and again allowed the lure to settle. Just like before, the lure came out of the pocket only to be swallowed up by another giant trout. The ensuing fight was exciting and Adrian landed the fish right next to the one already beached. "I remember looking around hoping someone would have seen this miracle. But it was just me, God, and two beautiful fish." He thanked God for these gifts and made his way back to his partner to share the joy and blessing.[1]

This event occurred over thirty years ago, but the sparkle in Adrian's eye as he shared the story testified that this was no ordinary trip. It was blessed of God. Adrian was a firm believer in the power of prayer and recognized that God loves His children enough to provide special gifts from time to time. While some may see Adrian's fishing adventure as a trivial thing to a God who created the universe, Adrian believed, "God doesn't see things as big or small. He hears the prayers of a small child with the same compassion and care as He listens to a great theologian."

OBEDIENT TO WHAT?

When I entered my teens, I began thinking about what I believed concerning God and religion. Not my parents' beliefs nor my friends, but what *I* really believed. There were a host of religions to choose from. In my family alone, we had Protestants, Catholics, and a number of Mormons. In addition, some Muslims had moved into our neighborhood along with the Jehovah's Witnesses who regularly knocked on our front door.

I soon learned that God has placed a void in every man's spirit that can only be filled by having a personal relationship with the Creator, the one who made us. Despite my liberal education, it just didn't make sense to believe there wasn't a Creator behind the universe. Both science and logic told me that there has to be more to life than what we experience on this earth.

Some of my young friends suggested that I "live life to the fullest," even if it meant getting into trouble, because there is no God. I endeavored to endorse the argument, but I ran into problems. An atheist takes the position that everything happens by chance. Somehow we developed from a one-cell organism that was swimming around in the sea and, through adaptation, evolved into what we are today. Even for a young teen, that concept seemed a little far-fetched.

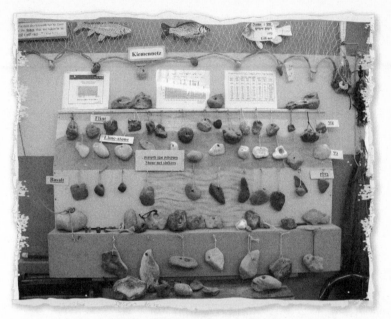

A display of boat anchors and net sinkers

I would ask, "Where did the sea come from?" and "What about the order I see in nature, the earth, and the universe?" and "If adaption and evolution made sense, why wouldn't there be apes occasionally having kids or lions or baboons?"

Okay, the atheist thing doesn't work. It's not logical, especially with all the scientists today who are now disputing the evolutionary theory. So I believe there is a God—now what? Who was this God-man named Jesus? An agnostic believes there is a god but doesn't necessarily believe that Jesus is the Son of God. Further, the agnostic would tell you that "something created all of this," but that "something" may or may not be God (as Christians define Him)—and either way, that "something" is certainly not involved in the lives of people. In other words, "something" started all of creation, and now just sits back and lets "nature" take its course. However, as I studied the life of Christ and evaluated foundational Christian literature, including the writings of ancient historians and renowned

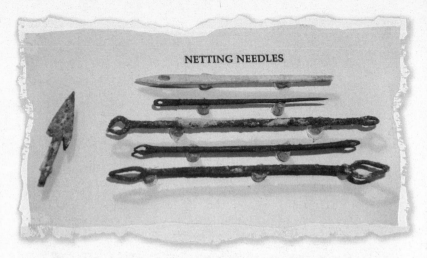

NETTING NEEDLES

Netting needles and tools that ancient fishermen used to mend their nets

theologians, I had to believe that a man named Jesus lived and was who He said He was—the Son of God.

In his masterful yet simple work *More than a Carpenter,* Josh McDowell states that, when you consider the evidence, historical record, prophecy, miracles, scientific proof, martyrs who died for their belief, claims of Christ, and the fact of His resurrection, you must settle on the most logical and best-defended position: He is our Lord! But perhaps you and I need a more definitive example. The late professor Peter Stoner (1883–1980), former Professor Emeritus of Science at Westmont College and Pasadena City College, stated the following in his book *Science Speaks*: "We find that the probability that any one man might have lived down to the present time and fulfilled (even) eight prophecies is 1 in 10 to the 17th power. That is one in 100,000,000,000,000,000."[2]

To enable us to better understand this staggering probability, Stoner illustrated it by supposing that we take 10 to the 17th silver dollars and lay them on the face of Texas. They will cover the entire state two feet deep. Now mark one of these silver dollars and stir the whole mass thoroughly all over the state. Blindfold a man and tell him he can travel as far as he wishes within the state, but he must pick up the marked silver dollar. Chances are 1 in 10 to the 17th power that he will pick up the correct silver dollar on the first try. That is the likelihood of one man fulfilling eight prophecies on his own. Jesus Christ fulfilled over 456 biblical prophecies![3]

BEING AN OBEDIENT FISHERMAN

In Luke, we find an amazing chapter about our fisherman disciples, as Jesus takes a potentially discouraging day and turns it into the best fishing day the disciples had ever experienced. The setting was along the shoreline of the Sea of Galilee. Jesus had been preaching and teaching all over Judea and the Galilee area. He had been rejected by His hometown crowd and moved toward Capernaum where the multitudes seemed to appreciate His teachings.

WHAT MAKES A GREAT FISHER OF MEN?

We come back to Luke 5:1–11 and the story of how Jesus used a fishing boat, a net, and His power to show the disciples a miracle they would remember for the rest of their lives. From God's Word, we find more truths that will transform our lives and help us with becoming spiritual mentors. A great fisher of men will demonstrate two very important characteristics: he will be obedient, even in small things; and he will have a prayerful heart.

1. OBEDIENT IN THE SMALL THINGS

Obedience is foundational to acting upon the truth we know. Knowing and obeying the gospel is how we act upon our faith. Although the disciples were tired and discouraged, they followed the requests of their Master. They pushed the boat off shore so Jesus would have a platform to speak from. The water reflected His voice so that all could hear. When Jesus asked them to put out into deeper water, after some initial discussion, they obeyed. This was a true test of

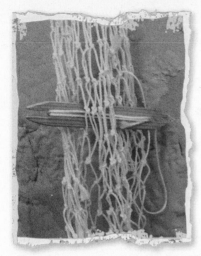

Model of ancient netting needle

obedience because any fisherman knows that you can't catch fish in the Galilee during the middle of the day, especially in deep water. Then Jesus asked them to let down their nets. Once again, the disciples responded with obedient hearts. Note the progression of trust and obedience.

Jesus didn't ask them right off to go out in the middle of the lake and cast their nets. As they showed their willingness to be obedient, God continued to direct and bless them. His blessing led to an overwhelming display of gratitude as well as embarrassment. Peter was so convicted by the miracle that he bowed down and asked to be alone so that he could work through his guilt. But Jesus knew his heart and quickly forgave the disciple for his lack of total trust. The disciples recognized His deity and began to refer to Him as "Lord" (v. 8), instead of master, teacher, skipper, or instructor as they had previously (v. 5).

If Peter had been only partially obedient, he would have missed the wonderful blessing God had in store for him. To be partially obedient is to be disobedient. Peter did *what* Jesus said, *when* He said to do it, and *the way* He said to do it. You and I are called to do the same.

2. AN OBEDIENT HEART IS A PRAYERFUL HEART

When the disciples asked Jesus, "Lord, teach us to pray," they uttered one of the deepest and most universal cries of mankind (Luke 11:1). Throughout the ages, men have sought to know God and have instinctively looked to prayer as the conduit through which they could dialogue with the Almighty. If we are to be truly obedient disciples, we must know what God is telling us to do. Reading His Word, fellowshipping with other mature believers, and praying form a strong three-legged stool for us to stand upon and reach up to God.

It is very interesting to observe the amount of literature presently on the bookshelves dealing with prayer. An old article from a major publication referred to prayer as "the most startling and encouraging scientific break-through of our era. . . . It can magically heal and prevent disease."[4] When you chat with people about prayer, it seems that almost everyone will state that they pray on occasion. Tragically, few people really approach the God of all creation with an earnest and expectant heart. Prayer for some has almost become a ritual or good-luck gesture.

LET'S GO FISHING

There are four types of prayer:

* **Petitionary**: Coming to God with specific needs that relate to you personally and can also relate to material possessions, better health, or the needs of others.

* **Conversational**: Speaking to God in your own words with your own thoughts. Because God is our Father, we can discuss our problems with Him as if He were our biological father.

* **Ritualistic**: Repeating a memorized prayer or reading a prayer from a book. Offering worship to God through the thoughts of someone else.

* **Meditative**: This involves moving beyond words or deeds to a reflective mind. By being still and waiting upon the Lord, He can guide you and provide a tremendous sense of well-being.

An effective prayer life is essential to being an obedient Christian. Even though Pastor Rogers has gone to be with Jesus, we can continue to hear his powerful messages through his radio and television ministry. When you hear Adrian Rogers pray or speak, you become convinced that his wonderful baritone voice must be similar to what Moses heard on the mountaintop. However, more important than his rich tonal qualities was his sincere and earnest desire to regularly communicate with the living God.

Dr. Rogers recognized that prayer is not only the refuge of the weak; it is the reinforcement of the strong. Prayer is not bending God's will to mine; it is bringing my will into conformity with God's. He can then work through me. Prayer should be regular and timely communication with God. If we truly want to experience His best, we must be in constant communication with Him about all things, big or small. And we must remember that prayer is a dialogue between two people who love each other. We must take the time to listen to the Father. He wants us to hear Him as much as He desires to hear us.

FISHING FOR MEN

If those observing our relationship with God see us actively communicating with our Lord, they will be more inclined to be engaged in prayer themselves. This is especially true with family members. Teaching others to confess, praise, worship, and then make their requests known to God is important in communicating with God. He delights in knowing that we recognize our sin and the saving grace we have because of His Son dying on Calvary's cross. He rejoices in our praise and worship as He patiently hears our needs, troubles, and challenges.

Are you regularly communicating with the God of all creation? How could you use prayer to assist those you are discipling? Prayer is opening the channels from our emptiness to God's fullness, from our self-centered ways to His desires for us to have a servant's heart, and from our defeat to His victory. How can you appropriate the power God has in store for you?

Read Matthew 6:6–14. Let us not pray like the hypocrites.

What does Psalm 51 say to you about prayer? What are the key words that will help you focus on an approach to your prayer life?

THE **DETERMINED** FISHERMAN

FISHING TALE

Fishing has always been more than just a sport. It originated at about the same time as hunting as a means of attaining food for survival. And from the beginning, this pastime has been one that requires determination. The first-century disciples were a model of determination. They would spend many nights a week casting their nets, oftentimes not catching a single fish (Luke 5).

Maybe one of the best fishing stories I've heard about a determined fisherman comes from our forty-first president, George H. W. Bush. During an August 1989 fishing vacation in Maine, President Bush went catchless for seventeen straight days. The eyes of the entire nation followed the daily events as reporters, photographers, and fishermen watched the president's every move in his twenty-eight-foot cigarette boat *Fidelity*.

The press declared a "fish watch" and used a bluefish with a red line through it to indicate each zero-fish day. Reporters were seen wearing improvised press credentials with a "no fish" logo. Several local fishermen and members of the press corps following the president would, on occasion, proudly wave *their* catch before the envious George Bush.

On the eighteenth day of his vacation, as a last resort, President Bush appealed to divine intervention by praying at St. Ann's Episcopal Church. That day, the president caught a ten-pound bluefish on a Jaw-Buster lure. Reporters, staff, Secret Service personnel, and local fishermen in nearby boats cheered the persistent fisherman. Back at the dock, the president was greeted with a hero's welcome for his triumph over a lone bluefish.

President Bush's story reminds us that determination is a key part of success in fishing, as it is in character building. Several decades before, an equally committed President Grover Cleveland described the virtues of such determination. "It is impossible to avoid the conclusion that the fishing habit, by promoting close association with Nature, by teaching patience, and by generating or stimulating useful contemplation, tends directly to the increase of the intellectual power of its votaries, and, through them, to the improvement of our national character."[1]

TOUGH TIMES

Another well-known Christian leader and fisherman who exemplifies determination is James Robison, a nationally known evangelist and missionary to thousands abroad. His courageous life demonstrates the type of character that is one of the by-products of being a determined warrior.

Life had been particularly tough for James's mother. She was a hard-working, practical nurse who was caring for an elderly man at his home in Houston, Texas. One night, the owner's son imposed his way and raped her. The result was an unwanted pregnancy. The forty-one-year-old woman decided that the best way to escape her situation was to abort the baby. After consulting with a few physicians, she was convinced instead to carry the child and offer it up for adoption. She put an ad in the paper and received a response from a Reverend and Mrs. Hale from Pasadena, Texas. This loving couple raised her son James with love and care until he was five. At this time in his life, James's mother, who never gave final adoption custody to the Hales, brought him home to live with her. Unfortunately, she hadn't much to offer her little boy, and they lived in very poor neighborhoods where James was regularly preyed upon by the local bullies.

Mosaic of fishermen holding cast-net 5th century

Robison recalls very few positive memories about his younger years, but cites among them a compelling sense of competition in sports and school. He remembers not being a great student but loving to read. "The teacher had a bookworm program going in fourth grade. . . . Somehow in the midst of all that reading, I developed some skills and even some admirable qualities."[2]

But for the most part, Robison experienced a sad, miserable childhood. "At the time I was so despondent, felt so worthless, that many nights I cried myself to sleep. I figured I was a bad boy, and that must be why I never got any breaks. No dad. No friends. No sports to play because I moved too many times. No loved ones who remembered me. Sometimes, when I was home alone, I banged my head against the wall until I knocked myself out. I just wanted to escape."[3]

Amidst all the negative, a few positive memories from James's early life shine through. He wrote fondly of his first exposure to nature, crediting his present avocation to a certain woman who invested in him at a young age. "Today I am a hunter and a conservationist because Timbo (a friend of an aunt) took the time to take me into the woods as a little boy. Somehow, she knew it was in me to want to spend time in the great outdoors. Hunting and fishing with her provided some of the most pleasant experiences of my childhood."[4]

WHAT MAKES A GREAT FISHER OF MEN?

Many single-parent young people (especially men) in our culture are desperately looking for a mentor-friend to help them understand the meaning of manhood. I provided chapels for some prisons and have often asked the inmates, "Do you think your life would have gone down a different path if you had a male role model and mentor?" I spoke with a chaplain at a California prison who said that 80 percent of those incarcerated did not have a biological father to provide guidance for life's decisions. It is not surprising that almost all of the men gave the same answer to my question: "If only I'd had someone to help direct my life."

James Robison's story speaks to the call for all of us to consider becoming a spiritual mentor to those kids in our churches and neighborhoods who don't have a dad at home. They aren't hard to find. If your church is not engaged in intergenerational ministries, it needs to be.

Shortly after high school, while attending a weeklong religious revival, Robison says he listened to the preaching, but felt he was far from God's ideal. "As I sat there, night after night, God was speaking to me, drawing me closer and closer to Himself. I found I was able to pray for the lost." It was then that he received a direct call from God, who he claims specifically told him to become an evangelist. "I knew God had called me. Beyond a shadow of a doubt, I fell so in love with Jesus that my heart overflowed. From that moment I had courage and compassion and zeal without measure. I didn't even

Larger mooring stone like these were also used as cultic idols (Shfifonim)

have anywhere to preach, but I was ready. I was willing. And because of God alone, I was able."[5]

Robison's first preaching experience came at a lunch break that he shared with two hundred other laborers as he stood atop a flatbed trailer. He could hardly believe his own ears as he began to share the love of Christ with these lost men whose minds were corrupted and filthy. "As the words tumbled out, I felt a boldness come over me, a sense of clarity of mind. I wasn't worrying about what people must be thinking of me. I was preaching!"[6]

But God didn't let him quit with two hundred, and soon he was preaching nationwide. "In one way, of course, I was not myself at all. If it had been me accepting those speaking invitations all over the United States, I would have stood before those people looking down at the floor, shuffling my feet, and mumbling. I was still shy and withdrawn. But when God gave me holy boldness, and taught me to use gestures, balance, and voice inflection, I became a different person in the pulpit. I felt comfortable. I stepped into the pulpit with confidence and righteous indignation over sin. I was forceful about the truths from the Word and emotional over the lost."[7]

TRUE SUCCESS

Robison overcame many hurdles to achieve success. His basic shyness was overcome through the gifting of God and a holy boldness. James preached over six hundred citywide crusades attended by more than twenty million people.

However, at a point in his life, the busyness of ministry began to undermine the godliness befitting a servant. It took a strong nudge from the Holy Spirit to remind him of a key to true success. "We thought nothing could stop us or even slow us down. Little did I realize that I had allowed the enemy an inroad: I was too busy, too successful for the intimate, personal devotion time with Jesus."[8] It was then that he learned that coming beside restful waters to be refreshed and loved by the Lord is a key to perseverance and true success. He began to pray that his own desires would never get in the way of God's will for his life. He went back to God's Word for wisdom instead of relying on life experiences for guidance. He pleaded with the Lord to remind him of his promise to always come back to Him in private, where it was just he and the Lord, loving each other. This encounter with God led him to great personal freedom and a commitment to spend time alone with God, some of that in the outdoors observing God's great creation.

Without a father growing up, there were precious few people who wanted to take a disenfranchised boy out fishing. As my relationship grew with God I realized he was the father I never had. He cared about what I cared about. He liked to see me have fun. I regularly called upon him for help in finding fish. He certainly knew what area of the lake to send Peter to (Matt. 17:24–27), and what side of the boat to tell the disciples to throw their nets (John 21:6).

On one occasion I had just finished a long and difficult mission trip to Africa. I decided to take a day off and go fishing. Even though it was in the middle of summer and the heat of the day, I felt confident. As I launched my boat I felt like I heard the Lord tell me, "James you did good, I know it was a hard trip and I want you to take your boat and go left, right through that little passage-way and cast over there to that little stump."

As my worm was sinking, I felt that "thud," I set the hook and this bass came out of the water spitting and sputtering. His mouth looked like a bucket. We played tug of war for a while then I scooped up this monster fish that weighed 11.2. As I was admiring the fish, I felt like I heard the Lord say, "How did you like that?"[9]

Whether fishing or ministering to the lost, James is always persevering. He is a focused individual who tries to constantly measure and evaluate situations to determine what is going to work. In the case of fishing, it is determining the equipment and strategy for that day; in the Christian life, it is distinguishing the voice of God and trusting it.

LET'S GO FISHING

I'm guessing that up to 40 percent of the people reading this book could share a similar story about longing for the love of a father. God put within us the need for a father's affirmation. Twice God gave His Son, Jesus, audible affirmation. When God's voice came down from heaven, His words penetrated the hearts of every man: "This is My beloved Son, in whom I am well pleased" (Matt. 17:5; see also Mark 9:7). I can hear the doubting voice of some who might say, "I'm not worthy enough for God to utter those words to me." My friend, that is why Jesus went to the cross—so that all of us could hear and accept those words.

What about those whose father abandons the family, or whose father has passed away, or for those who never received the affirmation of their dads? The psalmist testified of God's love when he stated that God is "a father of the fatherless" (Ps. 68:5). Don't let discouragement and loneliness overwhelm you. Recognize that your heavenly Father loves you so deeply and is guiding you through His Word, His Spirit, and your prayers. He is as close to you as this book.

Too often those of us who have a father's wound focus on what we don't have instead of on what we do have. We have the Spirit of God within us, we have the power of His Word, we are children of the King, and there is a spiritual mentor out there somewhere just for you.

Here is an inventory that might help you determine your calling:

1. Pray that God will show you a pathway to some occupation or ministry that aligns with His purpose and your gifting.

2. Find a good resource tool that helps you determine your spiritual gifts.

3. Talk to your pastor and close friends and ask them to identify what they think are your gifts, talents, and purpose so that you apply them with the greatest likelihood for success.

4. Try different things and see what God is telling you through the experience. Don't let initial failure or the fact that something is hard overwhelm you, and don't allow the success of your work to be determined by finances and attendance alone. Try and try again! Be a determined disciple.

5. Select a mentor who is not a critic but an encourager.

FISHING FOR MEN

What hurdles of pain and barriers has God helped you overcome? Can you imagine doing something that is worthwhile without struggles and some frustration? Most of us encounter some resistance when we are trying to explore God's purpose for our lives. Some people, including Satan, are robbers of joy. They want us to be discouraged and frightened about difficult challenges. Remember, we are in a spiritual battle that can manifest itself in a variety of ways.

Discuss with your mentoring partner what John 10:10 means and how it applies to your life.

What action will you take to find and apply your gifts and talents?

BE A
JOY-FILLED
ENCOURAGER

FISHING TALE

For more than three decades, many dedicated sportsmen have gathered round their television sets each week to watch their favorite fishing show host, Jimmy Houston. His wit and wisdom have entertained and challenged many aspiring anglers and hunters. Some would say he is one of the best fishermen in the world. There are those who would attest to his outstanding casting skills, while others might commend him for his entrepreneurship and ability to attract sponsors. If you hang around with Jimmy for any amount of time, you come away with a feeling that he has the personality of a clown, the energy of a centrifuge, the business mind of Donald Trump, and the compassion of your neighborhood minister. That is the Jimmy I know and love!

We have been friends for a very long time. It's been my pleasure to have worked with him as one of my board members while serving as executive director of the Fellowship Of Christian Anglers Society (FOCAS). We have filmed five television programs together, including episodes recorded while we were fishing the Sea of Galilee. I have viewed him closely under all kinds of pressure and circumstances. He is a remarkable icon who continues to inspire me with his honesty and passion.

*Mosiacs like this one from the 1st century are found in sites
around the Sea of Galilee*

Encouragement and joy are key components of Jimmy's personality, and the last two character traits we will consider in the closing chapters. When God gave out the encouragement pills and joy juice, Jimmy was first in line and received an ample supply of these blessings. The qualities I think of when I hear his name or see that Cheshire-cat grin underneath his shaggy blond hair are those of a child of God who has good cheer and encourages people through his "can do" attitudes.

It was no surprise, when I asked Jimmy for his all-time favorite fishing story, that he didn't tell me one of his personal exploits. Instead, Jimmy's favorite memory deals with the time he took his daughter Sherry along on a filming trip to Cato Creek Lake in Texas. Sherry had just turned twelve years old and was anxious to prove herself worthy of following in the footsteps of her mother, champion fisherwoman Chris Houston, who has won virtually every honor and tournament on the Ladies Bass circuit. She is the circuit's all-time money winner and has the respect and admiration of every fisherman.

As with most self-assured youth, Sherry didn't listen to dad regarding her choice of bait. Despite the fact that cameras were rolling and Jimmy was already working on his second limit, Sherry held firm on wanting to throw her favorite white spinner bait. "White bait is the right bait!" she shouted to Jimmy.

The old pro just kept smiling and chucking his blue and chartreuse single-blade spinner bait waiting to catch another fish and prove his daughter wrong—again. Suddenly, Sherry screamed, "Daddy, I've got a big one—I mean really big!"

Jimmy wasn't too excited until he saw the spunky bass shoot out of the water like a Polaris missile. This wasn't just any fish. It was a trophy largemouth that was giving Sherry a lesson in patience and perseverance. Sherry's screams and dad's shouts of encouragement filled the cove with excitement. Sherry was really afraid that she was going to lose her first trophy bass.

The drag peeled out the stretched line as her confidence grew. As the fat seven-pound bass approached the boat, Jimmy reached over and scooped it out by the lower jaw. The pride and excitement written on his face said it all.

WHAT MAKES A GREAT FISHER OF MEN?

I can only imagine the fun and character it took to be a fisherman in biblical days. One only needs to watch today's fishermen to see how they revel in the midst of their fishing duties. Even if it's your vocation, there is something inherently fun about catching a wary fish. So my friends, if you really want to become an effective spiritual mentor, you need to take a lesson from Sherry's story and take God seriously—but not yourself. Amidst the storms of life, the turbulence of our sick culture, and the fearful condition of our world, you must find time to encourage others with a joyful heart. My friend Jimmy certainly has found that combination to work.

A JOYFUL HEART IS A SERVANT'S HEART

As Jimmy recalled this wonderful story, I could sense the genuine joy in his heart—a joy that comes from a life filled with family and Jesus Christ. One would almost think that Jimmy and his family have never known hardship. He recognized early in his marriage and career that he needed to be a person who helps empower others to use their gifts and skills, especially with bashful people like his wonderful wife, Chris.

But the truth is that, on occasion, the strangling stresses of evil people have gripped his family, challenging their faith and threatening their happiness. I remember a time when Jimmy was constantly being harassed by an unfriendly company who tried everything to steal his joy and confidence. This stressful situation went on for years, yet Jimmy's heart never became faint as he continued to share his Spirit-filled life with all who came into contact with him. Despite the negatives going on in his own life, he was a consummate encourager to those around him.

Samuel Shoemaker said, "The surest mark of a Christian is not faith, or even love, but joy."[1] Jimmy's joy and ability to encourage others comes from knowing Jesus Christ as his personal Savior. His life is a testimony to the theory that joy is dependent upon Jesus, not the journey. Once you have Jesus in your heart, you can be an effective encourager. Despite the trials Jimmy encounters, he chooses to focus upon the positive aspects of life and his faith. This approach to life has formed an attitude of gratitude in Jimmy that results in a positive action plan for living.

I'm reminded of a story that fits positive people like Jimmy. There were two boys who were given a test. One boy was very rich and spoiled because everything had been given to him, although he was still not happy. A psychologist decided to run a test with this boy and a poor, destitute young man he was counseling. Knowing the rich boy's appreciation for the outdoors, the doctor placed him in a room filled with guns, bows, bass boats, and all the fishing gear you could imagine.

He took the poor boy, who had a positive outlook on life, and placed him in a dingy settling pond at the end of a sewage treatment plant giving him an old broken rod and reel with one lure tied on the frayed line. Several hours passed and the doctor went to the room where he had left the rich child, only to find him lying on the floor in tears because he was bored. He then went to the poor boy's settling pond, only to find the young man singing and running up and down the bank casting and shouting, "Where are you, Mr. Fish?" The doctor asked the boy what he was doing. The boy explained, "With all this cover and murky water, there must be a trophy bass in here somewhere!"

WHAT IS JOY?

Joy is an attitude characterized by a feeling of satisfaction, pleasure, and fulfillment. It is contentment and calmness resulting from a strong and abiding faith in the power and grace of the Almighty. Mother Teresa put it well: "Joy is prayer—Joy is strength—Joy is love—Joy is a net of love by which you can catch souls. . . . The best way to show our gratitude to God and to people is to accept everything with joy. A joyful heart is the inevitable result of a heart burning with love. Never let anything so fill you with sorrow as to make you forget the joy of the Christ risen."[2]

The word *joy* appears more than 150 times in the Bible. Joy is the cornerstone for our faith and witness to others. As you read these various verses, you recognize that joy is a deep inner peace that projects a sense of greater well-being and confidence.

Happiness, on the other hand, can be much more dependent on our circumstances. We are happy when the job promotion comes in on time. We feel cheerful when our financial dreams are met. We are glad when our favorite team wins a game and especially happy when they go to the Super Bowl six times. These feelings temporarily comfort a person—until the next trial or failure occurs. With happiness, there is no lasting or enduring significance to any event or material possession.

A joyful spirit has given Jimmy Houston the competitive edge in the many fishing and casting tournaments he has participated in. More importantly, joy has given Jimmy a philosophy for living. What is your approach to life? Can you think about being joyful?

Try listing three things that create real joy in your heart, not just happiness.

What is the nature of your joy? Is it family, faith-based issues, the ability to share Christ's love with others, living a Spirit-filled life, conquering fear or an addictive behavior, encouraging others—or is it directed more toward things?

LET'S GO FISHING

If the disciples were truly going to become *more than a fisherman*, they would need to find a joyful spirit in representing the Lord in their ministry. It would ultimately be their affectionate love, peace, faith, and joy that would draw people to them.

JOY IS FOUNDATIONAL TO OUR FAITH

It is natural to focus on the trials and struggles of daily life. For most of us, the pressures of our stress-filled environment create demands that can rip and tear at our character and spirit. For those of us who have sensitive and caring natures, we can often allow the critics and scoffers to pilfer moments of joy from our lives. Worry, fear, temptation, anger, and unresolved conflict are like thieves in the night that take every opportunity to steal away our delight. Certainly there was a lot of pressure on the first-century disciples. The serious nature of their calling and fate was etched into their minds every time Jesus chiseled away at their character.

As Jesus broke bread with His disciples during the celebration of His last Passover, He impressed upon them that His hour had come. He described His fate and continued to teach them important lessons about leadership, serving, sacrifice, and obedience. After imploring them to abide in His love, we hear His encouragement.

The House of Anchors is located along the Galilee shoreline in the Kibbutz Ein Gev. When you go to Israel put this stop on your itinerary. This building is filled with many fishing and boating artifacts.

"These things I have spoken to you, that My joy may remain in you, and that your *joy* may be full" (John 15:11, emphasis added).

Jesus wanted to see His joy remain in them, fill them, and totally consume them. If a disciple bears fruit and continues in love of Him, he will rejoice (have joy). Fruitful and faithful disciples are joyful servants. Christ's love will provide a continual feast to fill the hungry soul of any downhearted Christian. As the psalmist wrote, "They are abundantly satisfied with the fullness of Your house, and You give them drink from the river of Your pleasures" (Ps. 36:8).

Jesus said not to worry or fret. The opposite of worrying is to have a joy-filled life. "But seek first the kingdom of God and His righteousness, and all these things shall be added to you" (Matt. 6:33). What things are these that will be added? The basic needs of life, certainly, as that is the context of Matthew 6. But I believe that the Lord had much more in mind—specifically, as we pursue "the kingdom of God and His righteousness," God will develop in us the fruit of the Holy Spirit—and Paul tells us that this fruit includes joy. "But the fruit of the Spirit is love, joy, peace, longsuffering, kindness, goodness, faithfulness, gentleness, self-control. Against such there is no law" (Gal. 5:22–23).

If our hearts and minds are set on eternal issues, then our joy will come from knowing that the foundations of our faith are secure. Joy comes from knowing our eternal destiny and that this time on earth is like a drop of water in a huge lake. The real issue is, where will we spend eternity? If we have accepted Jesus Christ as our personal Savior, we have the guarantee of eternal life. The temporary struggles and pain we experience are just that: temporary.

Joy should also come in knowing we have the ultimate companion and friend who will never leave us or forsake us. The Holy Spirit is our comforter and guide who is never capricious or unfaithful. Even in difficult times, the Comforter can provide the inner peace required to maintain a deep and abiding joy.

We should receive encouragement and joy from friends and relatives who know that Christ will be with us forever. There will be no more good-byes, no more funerals, no loved ones moving away from home. The assurance that the kingdom of heaven is at hand for all who believe is a promise to be claimed and secured with joy.

People who know Jimmy Houston are amazed at his mental toughness, his competitive strength, and capability. One of the things that separates Christians from people who have had other "religious" experiences is our ability to receive energy from our joyful spirit. But without joy, the Christian faith cannot maintain its power. We can become motivated and fortified by our own commitment and through His power. "Do not sorrow, for the joy of the LORD is your strength" (Neh. 8:10).

JOY IS NOT DEPENDENT UPON OUR CIRCUMSTANCES

Throughout the writings of Paul, we are continually impressed with all his suffering. Trial after trial, we see Paul's faith tested, his body tortured, and his character assassinated. Yet, through it all, we also see his joy. Thirty-one times in Paul's writings he talks about his joy or being joyful or rejoicing. We see just one example of his teaching on joy in his letter to the Philippians. Note that he began and ended the following passage with comments on joy:

> What then? Only that in every way, whether in pretense or in truth, Christ is preached; and in this I *rejoice*, yes, and will *rejoice*. For I know that this will turn out for my deliverance through your prayer and the supply of the Spirit of Jesus Christ, according to my earnest expectation and hope that in nothing I shall be ashamed, but with all boldness, as always, so now also Christ will be magnified in my body, whether by life or by death. For to me, to live is Christ, and to die is gain. But if I live on in the flesh, this will mean fruit from my labor; yet what I shall choose I cannot tell. For I am hard-pressed between the two, having a desire to depart and be with Christ, which is far better. Nevertheless to remain in the flesh is more needful for you. And being confident of this, I know that I shall remain and continue with you all for your progress and *joy* of faith, that your *rejoicing* for me may be more abundant in Jesus Christ by my coming to you again. (Phil. 1:18–26, emphasis added)

Paul knew there would be trials, disappointments, threats, pain, and suffering. A Christian is not exempt from the testings of life. It's because we persevere and become approved that we will receive the crown of life, as mentioned in James 1:12. This, my friends, is why James could agree with Paul's teaching and say, "My brethren, count it all joy when you fall into various trials" (James 1:2).

Perhaps Mark Twain's thoughts help underscore this thought. "Grief can take care of itself; but to get the full value of a joy you must have somebody to divide it with."[3] We have the Holy Spirit and a caring, loving heavenly Father and the support of devoted Christians who will share and encourage us in both our trials and joy.

In order to help remind my friend Jimmy Houston of God's faithfulness, his wife, Chris, embroiders "Rejoice in the Lord always" (Phil. 4:4) on the back of all of his tournament fishing shirts. When Jimmy has had a particularly bad tournament, she hangs the shirt on the rearview mirror so he will see it when he gets into the van for the long trip home.

Are you denying or avoiding pain and trials? Don't avoid pain, suffering, and trials. They will refine your faith and can ultimately increase your joy. Remember, joy is refined and perfected in the crucible of trials (Psalm 45).

JOY RECOGNIZES THAT PAIN AND SUFFERING ARE PART OF LIFE

My good friend Tim Hansel, in his great book *You Gotta Keep Dancin'*, summarized how Christ prepared His disciples for the challenges beyond being a fisherman:

> If you can't change circumstances, change the way you respond to them. . . .
>
> God reminded me again and again that I cannot choose to be strong, but I can choose to be joyful. And when I am willing to do that, strength will follow. . . .
>
> Pain is inevitable, but misery is optional. . . .
>
> Joy is simple (not to be confused with easy). At any moment in life we have at least two options, and one of them is to choose an attitude of gratitude, a posture of grace, a commitment to joy.[4]

To focus on joy when undergoing trials is a matter of concentration. In the apostle Paul's life, we can see that it is a matter of fixation, and the target to focus on is the Lord Jesus. Just like a good fisherman, concentration is the key to being a joyful disciple. It is also the passport to victorious living. If our focus is fixed upon our circumstances, our pain, and our suffering, then it is difficult to have a joyful heart. But if our attitude is one of gratitude and joy, then our outlook will be positive and enriching.

JOY ENCOURAGES PEOPLE TO TAKE RISK

People who live with fear or despair tend to lock themselves into the known and predictable. Their lives can become stale and depressed without a fresh sense of excitement and vision. Paul encouraged the people of Philippi to be bold, to look beyond their circumstances with an expectant heart. "I eagerly expect and hope that I will in no way be ashamed, but will have sufficient courage so that now as always Christ will be exalted in my body, whether by life or by death" (Phil. 1:20 NIV).

Are you taking any risk today? Can you see the potential for joy when you stretch your faith? I can guarantee you that Jimmy Houston takes risks every day. He is out front on the firing lines of life willing to deal with the bullets and the pain.

JOY FLOURISHES IN TIMES OF SACRIFICE AND GIVING

Like every other tournament fisherman, Jimmy Houston loses more tournaments than he wins. I have been with him on several occasions when he didn't perform to his capabilities or his strategy was flawed. Despite his low standing at the end of the day, you can count on his spirit to be positive and energetic. Jimmy has discovered the secret of having a joyful Christian life. Like the psalmist, Jimmy believes we must "Be glad in the LORD and rejoice, you righteous; and shout for joy, all you upright in heart!" (Ps. 32:11).

Most anglers who have had a difficult tournament become embarrassed or frustrated with their lack of success. They will creep off to the nearest bar or lonely motel room to sulk in their despair. Jimmy chooses to be available to the fans, especially the kids, and seems to strengthen his joy with each and every contact. His smile and humorous self-criticism seem to take away his frustration and inspire the crowd of onlookers.

Simple as it seems, people who are joyful have learned to appreciate all the little things in life, and there truly are so many of them to choose from. Positive people tend to focus upon the possibilities of tomorrow rather than the defeats of today. I'm reminded of a sign that hangs proudly at a little fishing lodge on Lake Seminole in Georgia. It is meant to inspire and encourage anglers as they come and go. As you enter the property, the sign front reads "They tore 'em up yesterday." When you drive out, you see on the back side of the sign, "Cuz—I guarantee they'll bite tomorrow."

Are you looking to a positive future? Can you experience joy today, knowing that God's desire is to provide you a "good bite" tomorrow? As I observe Jimmy and reflect on what Scripture tells us about joy, I can see a few fundamental truths that will help each of us experience a more joyful life.

FISHING FOR MEN

What does it mean to be filled with joy? What do you suppose James meant when he said, "My brethren, count it all joy when you fall into various trials, knowing that the testing of your faith produces patience. But let patience have its perfect work, that you may be perfect and complete, lacking nothing" (James 1:2–4)?

What type of Christians appeal to you? Are you drawn to men who are cheerful and friendly, or do you prefer the more subdued and negative? Some of us take life more seriously and have difficulty always feeling joyful. What can we do to revel in the jubilant Spirit of our Lord?

Discuss with your mentoring partner how each of you could be a more joy-filled person. What is the difference between happiness (that is circumstantial) and joy (that is eternal)?

Read 2 Samuel 6. Why do you suppose King David was often dancing and singing as he worshipped God? What did he discover that brought him great joy?

THE POWER OF ENCOURAGEMENT

FISHING TALE

Maybe it was because I didn't feel much encouragement when I was a young boy that I value the opportunity to encourage others, yet I've since found that encouragement can be infectious and contagious. One of the joys our ministry has is working with children and military veterans who have disabilities. It was over thirty years ago that we started to encourage our volunteers to take their joy and passion into the field and utilize their love for others in a tangible way. By joint-venturing with service organizations and a major park district, we take from two hundred to five hundred disabled people to a local lake and connect them with compassionate men (fishing buddies)—and then, something special happens.

Each discipler or fishing buddy is matched with a disabled person and given instructions to help him have one of the best days of his life. Within four to five hours, they rotate through a stocked fishing area, lawn games, boat rides, and a nature study program. With a nice fish in their trophy bag, they proceed to a special lunch with their new friend.

What is amazing is the enthusiasm and encouragement you see with the participants. When one of the disabled people catches a fish, everyone on the shoreline roots him on. It is inspiring to see wheelchair-bound quadriplegics shout words of encouragement to their friends who are hooked up with a fish. And with the aid of some special electronic fishing gear, even those who cannot use their hands can reel a fish in on electronic reels strapped to their chest. The most hardened volunteer is often brought to tears as he senses the joy-filled environment.

Joy is often the by-product of encouragement, and it is spread in two directions: to the giver of encouragement, and to those who receive it. Who doesn't feel inspired hearing "that-a-boy!" Encouraging someone is a simple thing, yet it is often neglected in our self-centered culture. The "me generation" seems to place more emphasis on individualism than on teamwork. As Christians, however, we are instructed to be encouragers. Larry Crabb Jr. and Dan Allender, in their outstanding work on encouragement, wrote:

> Christians are commanded to encourage one another. Because words have the power to affect people deeply, it is appropriate to consider how to encourage fellow Christians through what we say. Words can encourage, discourage, or do nothing. We must learn to speak sincerely with positive impact, using our words to help other Christians pursue the pathway of obedience more zealously.[1]

The act of inspiring others should be fundamental to our faith. There are many lessons on encouragement in Scripture, but none more powerful than two from our Savior's life. Let's look at those two examples more closely.

WHAT MAKES A GREAT FISHER OF MEN?

As we mentioned before, on two separate occasions God the Father chose to publicly commend, inspire, and encourage His Son, Jesus. As an assembled crowd looked on, John the Baptist blessed and baptized Jesus in the Jordan River. God appreciated the moment and the willingness of Christ to apply Himself to the call. God the Father proclaimed, "This is My beloved Son, in whom I am well pleased" (Matt. 3:17). And again the same supporting message was proclaimed toward the end of His ministry as recorded by Matthew: "This is My beloved Son, in whom I am well pleased. Hear Him!" (Matt. 17:5).

Did Jesus the God-man really need to be encouraged? Probably not, but by way of modeling this principle, God provided the words of encouragement so we could see how important it is to our purpose and success. But what was God saying? It appears that these chosen words were intended to convey His support, approval, love, and acceptance. Perhaps He was saying something like, "I love you. I'm proud of you!"

THE PURPOSE OF CHRIST'S MINISTRY

Jesus could have used numerous passages of Scripture to announce His impending ministry, but He chose the book of Isaiah to emphasize the importance of encouragement. Shortly after returning to Galilee "in the power of the Spirit," He began His teaching at a synagogue in His hometown of Nazareth. He declared His mission and purpose by saying, "The Spirit of the Lord is upon Me, because He has anointed Me to preach the gospel to the poor; He has sent Me to heal the brokenhearted, to proclaim liberty to the captives and recovery of sight to the blind, to set at liberty those who are oppressed; to proclaim the acceptable year of the Lord" (Luke 4:18–19). Jesus was essentially saying, "I'm here to inspire, support, lift up, and encourage."

We all need encouragers, exhorters, coaches, helpers—people who sit in the balcony and root us on. Jesus came to inspire with courage. Through the written Word and the guidance of the Holy Spirit, Jesus can provide that ultimate inspiration and support that is so vital to fueling the motivation and stimulation needed for a creative life in Christ.

We all need encouragers and we should all be encouragers. The apostle Paul provides an excellent example of both. He received encouragement from a peer supporter named Barnabas. This exhorter emerged from the island of Cyprus and took on Paul as a primary disciple. There are those who would say that Barnabas was the "minister of encouragement," and in fact his name actually means "Son of Encouragement" (Acts 4:36). The lessons learned from Barnabas helped stimulate Paul's inspirational ministry and Paul's further mentoring of many others.

Because of the encouragement of their fishing buddies and surrounding friends, the disabled kids mentioned in the first section of this chapter accomplished something they never thought they could do. Do you want to be successful? Would you like a strong and respectful marriage and home? How do we build a winning team at home, at work, or within our church? The first step is to become an encourager!

LET'S GO FISHING

How did Jesus encourage Peter? Let's take a closer look at the relationship Jesus had with His disciples. His encouraging ways inspired and motivated these men to propel a ministry into the ages.

Fishermen by their nature tend to be optimistic. We think that every cast or throw of the net will produce fish. We look at every day and every fishing hole as an opportunity to learn more about our favorite sport. Yet even with all of our optimism, we sometimes feel the despair of failure and defeat. The fish seem to have more victories than we do. Fishermen seem to have greater "highs" and lower "lows" than most athletes. Despite our skill, much of our success depends on something that we really can't control: the bite of a fish.

A lot of fishermen seem to readily identify with Peter, in that his life was like a seesaw, full of ups and downs. Despite his struggles, Peter learned a great deal about encouragement from the relationship he had with Jesus. The book of Acts describes the encouraging power Peter had upon the fledgling church at Pentecost. He inspired and fostered spiritual growth in each person he connected with.

There are at least three things that we can learn about how to be an encourager from the relationship Jesus had with Peter:

encouragement starts at home, encouragement looks to the future and forgives the past, and encouragement doesn't abandon others. As you think about each of these concepts, challenge yourself to become a more inspirational disciple.

ENCOURAGEMENT STARTS AT HOME

Most scholars suggest that Jesus lived with Peter and his family for two of His three and a half years of ministry. Jesus could relate to Peter and his family in a special way. He knew that encouragement must start at home. Our Savior knew that His time was limited and that He needed to build a strong, supportive relationship with each of His disciples. Likewise, Scripture directs us to be encouragers of family. "Therefore, as we have opportunity, let us do good to all people, especially to those who belong to the family of believers" (Gal. 6:10 NIV). Who belongs to the "family of believers"? All who are followers of Jesus Christ are part of the "household of faith," as the New King James Bible words this verse. We are asked to encourage, but those we need to comfort the most are within our immediate family, those with whom we have a special intimacy.

Have you thought about having a chat with your pastor about creating a more supportive environment in your church? Maybe a group could be formed that would send birthday cards or get-well cards to each member. What about providing some encouragement to your pastors? Most likely they are some of the hardest-working people in the church who daily empty themselves into others. Who is pumping up their emotional tires? Maybe God is calling you to be that guy.

Jesus developed an encouraging relationship with each of His disciples, especially Peter. There was an intimacy that suggested a deep respect and admiration. Jesus called His disciples to that depth of commitment and relationship. Without a pledge of commitment, an encourager cannot be effective. The relationship has to first be built before encouragement can happen.

To have this type of relationship, we must have an abiding knowledge and allegiance to our families. We can only accomplish this by spending the time and effort it takes to be the ultimate encourager. I'm convinced that, if every home had an encouraging father, we could lessen our worry about gangs, suicides, drugs, teen pregnancy, and a host of other ills that plague our youth.

Just look what we are up against. In general, our culture is anything but encouraging. The media tells us that if we don't buy their products, we can't expect to smell good, have friends, keep our hair, and so on. The direct and indirect messages are, "You're a loser," "I'm better than you," and "Be a real man."

It seems that life can get most discouraging for our young people. Most psychologists tell us that a child needs ten positive affirmations for every negative message he receives in order to alleviate the effect negativism has on children.

God blessed us with twin sons. My wife and I determined that our home would be a place where our boys would feel supported and encouraged. For the most part, our words simply stated the same message that God gave Christ. To this day, we still sincerely tell them, "We love you and we are proud of you."

We are called to uplift one another. Regardless of our circumstances, may we continue to be strong and consistent encouragers—especially to our family. And the opposite is also true—that no matter what age, dads also need the encouragement of their families. For the most part, a successful and truly fulfilled man can be measured by the encouragement he receives from his family.

ENCOURAGEMENT LOOKS TO THE FUTURE AND FORGIVES THE PAST

Jesus is the ultimate encourager because He looks to the future and forgives the past. Christ's focus with Peter was not where this Galilean fisherman had been, but where he was going. Jesus had a vision, not of what he was, but of what he would become.

Think of Jesus' first conversation with Peter: "'You are Simon the son of Jonah. You shall be called Cephas' (which is translated, A Stone)" (John 1:42). Jesus looked deep within Peter to his very soul. He pointed to Peter's future, the future of being part of the foundation for the first-century church. Our Savior could see Peter's potential, who did in fact assume a leadership role at Pentecost.

How important is this "perspective of encouragement" to how we relate to others? It is everything. If people sense a genuine encouragement and support for their longings and dreams, they can be motivated to give their very best. People will respond to our expectations ladled with heaps of encouragement and joy. If we project a negative, discouraging future, people usually respond in kind. Encouragers often see considerable growth and commitment from individuals motivated by inspirational acts.

Fortunately for my wife and me, we received a word from God on this concept when we were young parents. Our boys were given the rich gift of music from God when they were six years of age. Louise and I endeavored to support them within their gifts and tried to "paint a bright future" as related to their real abilities. While there are some things we might have changed in the way we parented our children, this area of our support was undoubtedly significant.

DON'T ABANDON OTHERS

The "up and down" life of Peter can be seen time and time again in New Testament accounts. In Matthew 16, Jesus affirms Peter's faith and initial commitment as the "rock," only to rebuke him in verses 21–23 as "an offense." Then Peter denies Christ three times before His crucifixion. Despite his failures, Jesus continues to support Peter. At the end of His ministry on earth, Jesus asks Peter to reaffirm his love, then promptly encourages him and the other disciples in their future ministries.

We will all stumble and fall short. We will fail one another and God. Jesus did not abandon His disciples; He remained supportive and faithful. He never gave up on people, even at the cross. Neither will our Lord ever give up on you or me. He sent the Holy Spirit to minister to us and to be the ultimate supporter, comforter, and encourager. He regularly intercedes with the Father on our behalf (Rom. 8:34).

Remember, a committed encourager will exhaust all resources while continuing to try and motivate others. Jesus reached out to Peter as he was sinking (Matt. 14:28–31); He didn't let him go under. Encouragers need to regularly reach out to others and help pull them up. One of the best ways to help uplift individuals is to become a prayer warrior for those you wish to inspire. Prayer is powerful and will help unleash the power of God in the lives of people you pray for.

FISHING FOR MEN

What are some ways you can be an exhorter (encourager) of others? Read the following passages with your mentoring partner, and discuss how each demonstrates the art of encouraging others: Romans 15:4–9; Colossians 2:1–2; 1 Thessalonians 5:11; 2 Timothy 4:2; Philemon 1:7.

What is the model for blessing and encouragement that Jesus demonstrated in Mark 10:13–16? With your mentoring partner, discuss these examples that best illustrate how Jesus encouraged Peter:

1. Focus on the potential in others, not on past failures (John 1:40–42).

2. Help others when they are in a process of growth (Matt. 14:26–31).

3. Never give up on the relationship (Matt. 16).

AFTERWORD

I've known Jim Grassi for almost thirty years. He is not only a great fisherman but a guy who has a real heart to be a "fisher of men." As the host of Jimmy Houston Outdoors, I've enjoyed working with him on a few of our television episodes and in developing a national ministry directed to people who love God's outdoors.

In this book, Jim has helped us understand what Jesus was teaching His disciples. Through his experience as a fisherman, pastor, men's leader and confidant, Jim has presented many truths that stimulate us to a deeper understanding of what it means to be an authentic disciple (spiritual mentor). If ever there was a time we need to draw closer to God, it is now. We all need to fish for more truth and transparency that allows us to see God's purpose and plan for our lives.

Being a fisherman, storytelling comes easy for Jim. He is able to mix his knowledge of God's Word, fishing experience, wit, humor, and perspective into an enjoyable product that creates within us an appetite to be a true disciple of Christ. Yet this book isn't just for fishermen; it's directed to anyone who desires to grow closer to God.

The message contained within *More Than a Fisherman* calls each of us to think deeper about what it means to be a true disciple of Jesus. I encourage you to take some time to explore the questions scattered throughout the book. They will challenge you to become a better mentor to others.

Jimmy Houston
Host: *Jimmy Houston Outdoors*

GOD'S GAME PLAN FOR LIFE

Like a good fisherman developing a good plan for a special trip, our heavenly Father developed a plan for our salvation. He initially hoped man would connect with Him through His great creation—Adam and Eve thought they had a better idea. Then God utilized great patriarchs like Moses and Joshua to present His plan to His chosen people (the Jews), then great kings, priests, judges, and prophets, only to be saddened with the condition of man's prideful spirit and sin-filled heart. So how does our Great Guide God Almighty, get our attention? He sends in the best fisher-of-men and sacrifice of all time—Jesus Christ.

The Romans Road lays out the only game plan for salvation through a series of Bible verses from the book of Romans. These verses form an easy-to-follow explanation of the message of salvation.

The Romans Road clearly defines:

1. who needs salvation

2. why we need salvation

3. how God provides salvation

4. how we receive salvation

5. the results of salvation

THE ROMANS ROAD OF SALVATION

1. Everyone needs salvation because we have all sinned.

   As it is written: "There is none righteous, no, not one; there is none who understands; there is none who seeks after God. They have all turned aside; they have together become unprofitable; there is none who does good, no, not even one." . . . All have sinned and fall short of the glory of God. (Rom. 3:10–12, 23)

2. The price (or consequence) of sin is death.

   For the wages of sin is death, but the gift of God is eternal life in Christ Jesus our Lord. (Rom. 6:23)

3. Jesus Christ died for our sins. He paid the price for our death.

> But God demonstrates His own love toward us, in that while we were still sinners, Christ died for us. (Rom. 5:8)

4. We receive salvation and eternal life through faith in Jesus Christ.

> That if you confess with your mouth the Lord Jesus and believe in your heart that God has raised Him from the dead, you will be saved. For with the heart one believes unto righteousness, and with the mouth confession is made unto salvation. . . . For "whoever calls on the name of the LORD shall be saved." (Rom. 10:9–10, 13)

5. Salvation through Jesus Christ brings us into a relationship of peace with God.

> Therefore, having been justified by faith, we have peace with God through our Lord Jesus Christ. (Rom. 5:1)

> There is therefore now no condemnation to those who are in Christ Jesus. (Rom. 8:1)

> For I am persuaded that neither death nor life, nor angels nor principalities nor powers, nor things present nor things to come, nor height nor depth, nor any other created thing, shall be able to separate us from the love of God which is in Christ Jesus our Lord. (Rom. 8:38–39)

RESPONDING TO THE ROMANS ROAD

If you believe the scriptures in Romans lead to the path of truth, you can respond by receiving God's free gift of salvation today. Here's how:

1. Admit you are a sinner.

2. Understand that as a sinner, you deserve death.

3. Believe Jesus Christ died on the cross to save you from sin and death. Believe that He conquered death itself when He rose from the grave.

4. Repent by turning from your old life of sin to a new life in Christ.

5. Receive, through faith in Jesus Christ, His free gift of salvation.

ADDITIONAL RESOURCES

For additional resources or assistance, please e-mail Men's Ministry Catalyst at www.mensministrycatalyst.org.

FISHING FOR SOULS

Any realtor would tell you that the three most important things associated with selling or purchasing a home are location, location, location. An effective spiritual mentor would say that after praying that the Holy Spirit prepares a person's heart for your offerings, the most important element of building a relational bridge to unchurched folks is to pick the right time, the right place, and the right approach. These things are most important to developing a trusting relationship. Remember that God is your spiritual guide and you are the assistant guide.

Meditate on these verses before you select an idea that creates a bonding memory with the person you are leading to Christ.

> Your word is a lamp to my feet
> And a light to my path. (Ps. 119:105)

> You in Your mercy have led forth
> The people whom You have redeemed;
> You have guided them in Your strength
> To Your holy habitation. (Ex. 15:13)

> Then you will understand righteousness and justice,
> Equity and every good path.
> When wisdom enters your heart,
> And knowledge is pleasant to your soul. (Prov.
> 2:9–10)

Sports and the outdoors are excellent bridge-building ways to connect with an unbeliever. But first, learn from one another. Obviously you don't take someone out hunting until you know his capabilities and concerns about safety.

* Plan an outing together: fishing trip, hunting trip, rafting, outdoor photography, biking, hiking, camping, horseback riding, golfing, archery, shooting sports, or skiing.

* Attend a sports event together: basketball, football, hockey, baseball, golf tournament, auto racing, or snow sports.

* Invite them to join you at a fair, sports show, auto show, or clinic.

Build relationships through shared interest in things that are inexpensive and don't require an all-day commitment. Remember, most often the way to a man's heart is through things involving food, humor, fun, and exciting opportunities to grow in his knowledge or make him look good. Consider activities such as a barbeque, a trip to the flea market, concerts, plays, going out to dinner, community events, a street fair, or perusing a computer store, sports store, or hardware store.

Oftentimes actions speak louder than words. Consider doing a chore together for a neighbor or friend who either temporarily doesn't have the health to do it or is not physically able to handle a tough task like lawn mowing, snow removal, and other handyman stuff. You can also just check in on how he is doing with keeping up the house.

Your church could hold a car clinic for single-parent moms, a workday, a program for disabled kids, an outdoor adventure fair, or tutorial programs for high-risk kids. Usually anything involving helping kids is a winner.

I encourage you to obtain my book *Building a Spiritual Mentor*, published by Thomas Nelson, for specifics on the above ideas and for a host of other practical ways to reach the unchurched man.

ACKNOWLEDGMENTS

I praise God for the many relationships, experiences, and wisdom He has given me to formulate the concepts within this work. When Jesus said, "Follow Me, and I will make you fishers of men" (Matt. 4:19), He started a revival of spirit and hope that changed the world. Shortly thereafter, men began to gather together for worship and fellowship.

Isn't it interesting that when Jesus started His ministry, He picked eight fishermen to be among the initial twelve. He knew that the same passion, zeal, and perseverance that inspired His fishermen to be successful in catching fish would now be utilized to catch men, women, boys, and girls who would follow His Word. Our Lord's inspiration to His disciples helped them know the importance of knowing God and making Him known. If twelve common men could impact the world for Christ's sake, what can we do with the power of the Holy Spirit and the many resources available to us today? The power of His Word cannot be denied.

In my study of Scripture, there are three places that helped me better understand the importance of what it means to be a disciple (spiritual mentor): Matthew 28, Matthew 4:17–20, and Romans 12. In this work, I have discussed how each of these timely scriptures helped shape my perspective and mission when it comes to living out my faith.

As our Lord began His teaching, He challenged His followers with these words: "The time is fulfilled, and the kingdom of God is at hand. Repent, and believe in the gospel" (Mark 1:15). Certainly the fulfilling of biblical prophecy suggests that, for believers, the kingdom of heaven is nearer today than it was at the time of Christ. Are you ready for His return? I hope you are and that this work might help you better appreciate a believer's role and challenge during the end-times.

I greatly appreciate the patience and grace given to me by my wonderful wife, Louise, and by the talented Men's Ministry Catalyst team. Undertaking the writing of five books within an eighteen-month period—while still maintaining my role in full-time ministry—was a task I won't repeat. I'm thankful for the health, strength, and vitality God gave me to complete the tasks set before me.

I'm especially indebted to all our ministry partners, supporters, and board members who have faithfully served and supported our ministry and me during our thirty-three years of serving our Lord.

I greatly appreciate the assistance and cooperation I received from Yoel Ben-Yosef, Beit Haoganim (The House of Anchors) Museum at Kibbutz Ein Gev, Sea of Galilee, Israel and the late Mendel Nun for their help in providing many of the photographs. God bless you and Israel!

Finally, I want to once again thank the gifted staff and editors with Thomas Nelson for their encouragement and work involved with all my projects. As Scripture reminds us, "Grow in the grace and knowledge of our Lord and Savior Jesus Christ. To Him be the glory both now and forever. Amen" (2 Peter 3:18).

ABOUT THE AUTHOR

Dr. Jim Grassi is an award-winning author, communicator, outdoorsman, pastor, and former television cohost. He has presented hundreds of messages and programs around the world that helped equip people to fulfill the Great Commission (Matt. 28). He brings a sense of challenge, wisdom, excitement, and humor to his presentations, as he connects with people of various cultures and backgrounds. Through his multimedia outreach ministry, he encourages participants toward a greater understanding and appreciation of evangelism, discipleship, and the development of creating vibrant men's ministries. His practical approach to teaching biblical truth has captivated audiences around the world.

Jim Grassi is the founder and president of the culturally strategic Men's Ministry Catalyst, an organization he incorporated in 1981. Grassi is also the author of several books, including *The Ultimate Fishing Challenge, Heaven on Earth, In Pursuit of the Prize, The Ultimate Hunt, Crunch Time, A Study Guide of Israel, The Ultimate Men's Ministry Encyclopedia, Crunch Time, Crunch Time in the Red Zone, Guts, Grace, and Glory—A Football Devotional, The Spiritual Mentor,* and *Building a Ministry of Spiritual Mentoring.* Jim has also written numerous magazine articles, booklets, and tracts.

Dr. Grassi has appeared on many radio and television programs including *Hour of Power, The 700 Club, The Carol Lawrence Show,* Cornerstone Television, Southern Baptist Television—*Cope,* Chicago Television 38, *The Dick Staub Show, Getting Together, In-Fisherman, Fishing Tales, Jimmy Houston Outdoors, Home Life,* FOX Sports, and CSN.

Dr. Grassi was born and reared in the San Francisco Bay area. Known for his evangelistic heart, he teaches people from a background of an outdoorsman, public administrator, Hall of Fame fisherman, college professor, businessman, community leader, and pastor. He has served in the capacity of a chaplain with the San Francisco 49ers, the Oakland Raiders, Hurricane Katrina relief efforts, and the Post Falls, Idaho Police Department. His life experiences, study of discipleship, and work with hundreds of churches has given him a unique perspective on helping men to know God and make Him known.

RESOURCES AVAILABLE

Men's Ministry Catalyst: Resources available through MMC at www.mensministrycatalyst.org.

Weekly Devotionals for Men at www.mensministrycatalyst.org/stay-informed/devotional-archives/: Ideal for pastors and men's leaders to e-mail to their men.

MMC Library of Best Practices: Especially designed to assist leaders, available at (208) 457-9619.

MMC Hotline (208) 457-9619: Call anytime for assistance on creating ministry to men.

Monthly Men's Ministry Newsletter: This monthly e-mail newsletter provides tips and techniques on how to equip, inspire, and motivate men for kingdom purposes, available at www.mensministrycatalyst.org.

Dr. James Grassi as a speaker, coach, and equipper for individuals, men's leaders, and churches. Find more information at www.romans12disciple.org.

SOCIAL MEDIA

http://www.mensministrycatalyst.org/blog

http://www.romans12disciple.org

http://www.facebook.com/MensMinistryCatalyst

http://twitter.com/MensMinCatalyst

http://www.youtube.com/user/MensMinCatalyst

Personal Church Consulting: We will send a church consultant to your location; call (208) 457-9619.

Men's Ministry Assessment Survey: We have the capacity to customize, process, and evaluate your survey.

Conferences and Retreats: Our extensive experience in providing speakers, logistics, and support for your men's retreats, conferences, and special events. Call (208) 457-9619.

Speakers Bureau: A list of qualified national speakers and sports personalities to enhance your programs. Call (208) 457-9619.

Primary Provider of Iron Sharpens Iron programs on the West Coast: (208) 457-9619.

NOTES

INTRODUCTION

1. Phil Downer, *Eternal Impact* (Eugene, OR: Harvest House, 1997), 13–14.
2. Bob Horner, Ron Ralston, and David Sunde, *The Promise Keeper at Work* (Nashville: Thomas Nelson, 2005), 103.

CHAPTER 1

1. Peter Marshall speech at the University of Pittsburgh, 1946.
2. Washington Area Coalition of Men's Ministries, "Why Men Matter—Both Now and Forever: A Look at the Numbers About Men and Men's Ministry," www.wacmm.org/stats.html, accessed December 17, 2013.
3. Kenneth Bradwell, executive director, Fathers Incorporated. "Child Support Report," Office of Child Support Enforcement, Vol. 33, No. 6, June, 2011.
4. Jim Grassi, *Heaven on Earth* (Eugene, OR: Harvest House, 1970), 28.
5. Dietrich Bonhoeffer, *The Cost of Discipleship* (New York: Touchstone, 1995), 57, 59.

CHAPTER 2

1. Jim Grassi, *The Spiritual Mentor* (Nashville: Thomas Nelson, 2013), 104.
2. Joseph Henry Thayer, *Greek-English Lexicon of the New Testament* (New York: Harper Brother, 1899), 389.
3. Pat Morley, *Pastoring Men: What Works, What Doesn't, and Why It Matters Now More than Ever* (Chicago: Moody, 2009), 78.

CHAPTER 3

1. David Needham, *Close to His Majesty* (New York: Doubleday, 1990), 14.

CHAPTER 5

1. Bill Hull, *Jesus Christ, Disciplemaker* (Grand Rapids: Baker, 2004), 85.

CHAPTER 6

1. Douglas S. Ritter, Equipped to Survive Foundation, http://www.equipped.org/stop.htm, accessed October 29, 2013. Used by permission.
2. E. Stanley Jones, *How to Pray* (Nashville: Abingdon, 1979), 5.

3. Ibid, 6.
4. Ibid.

CHAPTER 7

1. Charles R. Swindoll, *Swindoll's Ultimate Book of Illustrations and Quotes* (Nashville: Thomas Nelson, 1998), 38.
2. *McGuffey's Third Eclectic Reader* (New York: American Book Co., 1920), 151.
3. Gordon MacDonald, *Restoring Your Spiritual Passion* (Nashville: Oliver-Nelson, 1986), 18.
4. Ibid, 30.
5. J. B. Phillips, *Your God Is Too Small* (New York: Touchstone, 2004), 56.
6. John Wesley, *The Works of the Reverend John Wesley, A.M.* (New York: J. Emory and B. Waugh, 1831), 784.

CHAPTER 8

1. Charles R. Swindoll, *Laugh Again* (Nashville: Thomas Nelson, 1992), 40.

CHAPTER 9

1. Mendel Nun, *The Sea of Galilee and Its Fishermen in the New Testament* (Ein Gev, Israel: Kibbutz Ein Gev Publishing, 1989), 28–34.
2. Ibid., 23–27.
3. Ibid., 16–22.

CHAPTER 10

1. Personal conversation with Dr. Adrian Rogers, October 14, 1996, Memphis, TN.
2. Peter W. Stoner, *Science Speaks* (Chicago: Moody, 1963), 107.
3. Ibid.
4. Raymond Finch, *The Power of Prayer* (Boca Raton, FL: Globe Communications, 1996), 5, 47.

CHAPTER 11

1. Grover Cleveland, *Fishing and Shooting Sketches* (New York: The Outing Publishing Co., 1906), 96–97.
2. James Robison, *Thank God, I'm Free* (Nashville: Thomas Nelson, 1988), 19–20.
3. Ibid, 26–27.

4. James Robison, *Knowing God as Father* (Fort Worth, TX: Life Today, 1996), 22–23.

5. James Robison, *Thank God, I'm Free*, 58, 60.

6. Ibid, 63.

7. Ibid, 71–72.

8. Ibid, 90.

9. Personal conversation with James Robison, 1997, New Zealand.

CHAPTER 12

1. Martin H. Manser, ed., *The Westminster Collection of Christian Quotations* (Louisville, KY: Westminster John Knox Press, 2004), 241.

2. Mother Teresa, *A Gift for God: Prayers and Meditations* (San Francisco: HarperCollins, 1996), 77.

3. Mark Twain, *Following the Equator* (Hartford, CT: American Publishing Company, 1897), 447.

4. Tim Hansel, *You Gotta Keep Dancin'* (Elgin, IL: David C. Cook, 1985), 37, 47, 55.

CHAPTER 13

1. Lawrence J. Crabb Jr. and Dan B. Allender, *Encouragement* (Grand Rapids: Zondervan, 1984), 25.